FIRST PAST THE POST®

Mathematics:

Crosswords

Puzzles

Book 1

About the authors

The Eleven Plus Exams' **First Past The Post®** series has been created by a team of experienced tutors and authors from leading British universities including Oxford, Cambridge and Imperial College London.

Published by Technical One Ltd t/a Eleven Plus Exams.

With special thanks to the children who tested our material at the Eleven Plus Exams centre in Harrow.

ISBN: 978-1-912364-50-3

Copyright © ElevenPlusExams.co.uk 2017

All rights reserved. No part of this publication may be reproduced, stored or introduced into a retrieval system or transmitted in any form or by any means, without the prior written permission of the publisher nor may be circulated in any form of binding or cover other than the one in which it was published and without a similar condition including this condition being imposed on the subsequent publisher.

About Us

At ElevenPlusExams we supply high-quality, specialist 11 plus tuition for your children. Our website at **www.elevenplusexams.co.uk** is the largest in the UK that specifically prepares children for the 11 plus exams. We also provide online services to schools and *Our First Past the Post* range of books has been well-received by schools, tuition centres and parents.

ElevenPlusExams is recognised as a trusted and authoritative source. We have been quoted in numerous national newspapers, including *The Telegraph*, *The Observer*, *The Daily Mail* and *The Sunday Telegraph*, as well as on national television (BBC1 and Channel 4), and BBC radio.

Our website offers a vast amount of information and advice on the 11 plus, including a moderated online forum, books, downloadable material and online services to enhance your child's chances of success. Set up in 2004, the website grew from an initial 20 webpages to more than 65,000 today, and has been visited by millions of parents. It is moderated by experts in the field, who provide support for parents both before and after the exams.

Don't forget to visit **www.elevenplusexams.co.uk** and see why we are the market's leading one-stop shop for all your 11 plus needs. You will find:

- ✓ Comprehensive quality content and advice written by 11 plus experts
- ✓ ElevenPlusExams online shop supplying a wide range of practice books, e-papers, software and apps
- ✓ Lots of FREE practice papers to download
- ✓ Professional tuition service
- ✓ Short revision courses
- ✓ Year-long 11 plus courses
- ✓ Mock exams tailored to reflect those of the main examining bodies

Other titles in the First Past The Post® Series

VERBAL REASONING

ISBN	TITLE
978-1-912364-60-2	Verbal Reasoning: Cloze Tests Book 1 - Mixed Format
978-1-912364-61-9	Verbal Reasoning: Cloze Tests Book 2 - Mixed Format
978-1-912364-62-6	Verbal Reasoning: Vocabulary Book 1 - Multiple Choice
978-1-912364-63-3	Verbal Reasoning: Vocabulary Book 2 - Multiple Choice
978-1-912364-64-0	Verbal Reasoning: Vocabulary Book 3 - Multiple Choice
978-1-912364-65-7	Verbal Reasoning: Grammar and Spelling Book 1 - Multiple Choice
978-1-912364-66-4	Verbal Reasoning: Grammar and Spelling Book 2 - Multiple Choice
978-1-912364-68-8	Verbal Reasoning: Vocabulary in Context Level 1
978-1-912364-69-5	Verbal Reasoning: Vocabulary in Context Level 2
978-1-912364-70-1	Verbal Reasoning: Vocabulary in Context Level 3
978-1-912364-71-8	Verbal Reasoning: Vocabulary in Context Level 4

ENGLISH

978-1-912364-02-2	English: Comprehensions Classic Literature Book 1
978-1-912364-05-3	English: Comprehensions Contemporary Literature Book 1
978-1-912364-08-4	English: Comprehensions Non-Fiction Book 1
978-1-912364-17-6	Creative Writing Examples
978-1-912364-14-5	English: Mini Comprehensions - Inference Book 1
978-1-912364-15-2	English: Mini Comprehensions - Inference Book 2

NUMERICAL REASONING

978-1-912364-30-5	Numerical Reasoning: Quick-Fire Book 1
978-1-912364-31-2	Numerical Reasoning: Quick-Fire Book 2
978-1-912364-32-9	Numerical Reasoning: Quick-Fire Book 1 - Multiple Choice
978-1-912364-33-6	Numerical Reasoning: Quick-Fire Book 2 - Multiple Choice
978-1-912364-34-3	Numerical Reasoning: Multi-Part Book 1
978-1-912364-35-0	Numerical Reasoning: Multi-Part Book 2
978-1-912364-36-7	Numerical Reasoning: Multi-Part Book 1 - Multiple Choice
978-1-912364-37-4	Numerical Reasoning: Multi-Part Book 2 - Multiple Choice

MATHEMATICS

978-1-912364-43-5	Maths: Mental Arithmetic Book 1
978-1-912364-45-9	Maths: Worded Problems Book 1
978-1-912364-46-6	Maths: Worded Problems Book 2
978-1-912364-47-3	Maths Dictionary Plus

NON-VERBAL REASONING

978-1-912364-85-5	3D Non-Verbal Reasoning Book 1
978-1-912364-86-2	3D Non-Verbal Reasoning Book 2
978-1-912364-87-9	2D Non-Verbal Reasoning Book 1
978-1-912364-88-6	2D Non-Verbal Reasoning Book 2

PUZZLES

978-1-912364-50-3	Maths Crosswords Book 1
978-1-912364-51-0	Maths Crosswords Book 2
978-1-912364-74-9	Verbal Reasoning Vocabulary Puzzles Book 1
978-1-912364-75-6	Verbal Reasoning Vocabulary Puzzles Book 2

TEST PAPER PACKS

978-1-912364-00-8	English Practice Papers - Multiple Choice Pack 1
978-1-912364-48-0	Mathematics Practice Papers - Multiple Choice Pack 1
978-1-912364-76-3	Verbal Reasoning Practice Papers - Multiple Choice Pack 1
978-1-912364-83-1	Non-Verbal Reasoning Practice Papers - Multiple Choice Pack 1

Contents

This workbook comprises 35 crosswords, 27 of which cover core topics, and eight of which cover a mixture of topics.

Instructions

Across:

1 Decrease 238 by 119. (3)

3 Six hundred and fifty-eight minus one hundred and eighty-five. (3)

6 174 + 127 (3)

7 Textbook one costs £38 and textbook two costs £56. If both textbooks are purchased together, there is a £15 saving off the total price. How much would purchasing both books cost if bought together? (2)

Down:

1 Amar received 374 emails one week. How many more than 197 emails was this? (3)

2 Marissa took 1 hour and 3 minutes to finish her first piece of work. She then worked on a second piece for 29 minutes. How long did she spend in total on her work in minutes? (2)

3 What is the sum of 43, 90, −35, 387 and 2? (3)

- The numbers in red on the left hand side of the questions correspond to the small numbers already in the crossword.

- The number in brackets at the end of each question refers to how many digits are in the answer.

- Your child should complete the crosswords without the aid of a calculator.

- They should use additional paper for any working out.

- Answers are provided at the back of the book.

- Have fun!

BLANK PAGE

FIRST PAST THE POST®

Crosswords

Crossword 1: Addition and Subtraction

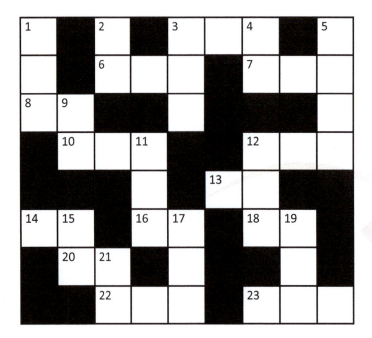

Across:

3 Deduct 71 from 218. (3)

6 What is the sum of the values in the circles? (3)

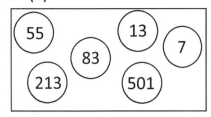

7 219 + 491 (3)

8 What is the difference between 1,896 and 1,915? (2)

10 Shop A has 174 magazines and Shop B has 452 magazines. How many magazines do shops A and B have altogether? (3)

12 How many over 1,032 is 1,297? (3)

13 29 − (−21) (2)

14 Beth buys a sandwich for £2, a drink for £1, biscuits for £1 and grapes for 49p. How much change, in pence, does Beth receive if she pays with a £5 note? (2)

16 What is the sum of −14 and 61? (2)

Down:

1 Increase 85 by 26. (3)

2 If 108 + N = 188, what is 108 − N? (2)

3 Subtract 7,360 from 7,480. (3)

4 How many fewer than 205 is 128? (2)

5 What is three thousand, nine hundred and seventy-eight plus two thousand, one hundred and seven? (4)

9 How much lower is 76 than 172? (2)

11 Ben collects stickers. He has 282 of the 1,081 he needs. His friend Amy gives him 195 more stickers, all of which are different from the ones he has. How many more stickers does Ben require to complete his collection? (3)

12 A film lasts for exactly three hours excluding advertisements, which last for 24 minutes. How long are the film and the advertisements in total, in minutes? (3)

15 The height of Television A is 21 inches and the height of Television B is 32 inches. What is their height difference in inches? (2)

Across:

18 7 + 7 + 7 + 7 + 7 + 7 + 7 (2)

20 Reduce £39 by £22 giving your answer in pounds(£). (2)

22 23 + 219 – 0 – 87 + 49 (3)

23 On Monday 384mm of rain fell. On Tuesday, 91mm of rain fell. What was the difference in rainfall between the two days, in mm? (3)

Down:

17 21335 – 20621 (3)

19 What is the difference between the largest two values below? (3)

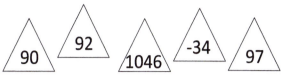

21 How many more is 864 than 792? (2)

Working out:

Crossword 2: Multiplication and Division

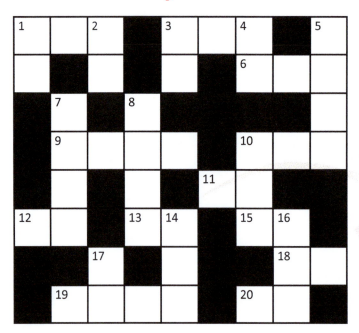

Across:

1 Find the product of 11 and 22. (3)

3 A large container holds 80.4 litres of water. How many 200 millilitre bottles could be filled using the water in the container? (3)

6 Max has 17 fifty pence coins in his pocket. How much money is this in pence? (3)

9 A DVD player costs £29. How much would 329 DVD players cost in pounds (£)? (4)

10 A tree is four times higher than a hedge. If the hedge is 2.2 metres in height, how high is the tree in cm? (3)

11 Lewis bought 14 boxes of eggs. Each box contained 6 eggs. How many eggs did Lewis buy? (2)

12 Ninety six biscuits are to be shared equally between 6 people. How many biscuits will each person receive? (2)

13 What would 115 pencils cost if 140 pencils cost £84? Give your answer in pounds(£). (2)

Down:

1 £504 is split equally between 18 people. How much does each person receive in pounds(£)? (2)

2 A number is multiplied by 7 to give 161. What is the number? (2)

3 882/21 (2)

4 A banana costs 13 pence. How many bananas could be bought with £3.64? (2)

5 120 × 25 (4)

7 What is the quotient when 19,904 is divided by 4? (4)

8 Becky ran for 36 minutes every day for 96 days. How long did she spend running in total, in minutes? (4)

10 2 × (−8) × (−53) (3)

14 Three thousand six hundred and sixty footballs are to be shared equally between four teams. How many footballs will each team receive? (3)

Across:

15 Emma is 14.5 times older than Jai. If Jai is 6 years old, how old is Emma in years? (2)

18 What is the result of multiplying the number of black squares by the number of circles? (2)

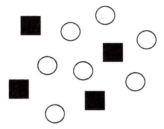

19 203 × 5 (4)

20 1,188 ÷ 12 (2)

Down:

16 What is the result of multiplying 9 by itself 3 times? (3)

17 How many hours are equivalent to 180,000 seconds? (2)

Working out:

Crossword 3: Mixed Operations

Across:

1 Jake bought four watches, each priced at £16 and six tennis balls, each priced at £2. How much did he spend in total, in pounds(£)? (2)

2 15,700 marbles were shared equally between five people. One of the five people, Wai already had 999 marbles. How many marbles does Wai now have? (4)

6 Tomba opens a new 1.5kg bag of sugar. He puts one quarter of the sugar in an empty jar. From the jar he uses two thirds of the sugar to bake a cake. How many grams of sugar are left in the jar? (3)

7 What is the difference between the product of 27 and 38 and the product of 110.5 and 8? (3)

9 A room is 2.5m in height. A table stands on the floor and is 500mm in height. How many boxes of height 12.5cm could be stacked on top of each other on the table? (2)

Down:

1 Janet ran four miles. Each mile took her 11 minutes to complete. She then drove for ten miles and each mile took 3.5 minutes to complete. How many minutes in total did she spend on these two activities? (2)

3 44mm was taken off the end of a 33cm bread stick and thrown away. The rest of the bread was cut into 22 equal parts. What was the length of one part, in mm? (2)

4 $[56 \times (6 + 27)] \div 2$ (3)

5 $(2{,}335 - 367) \div (6 \times 4)$ (2)

6 16.74×100 (4)

7 $(-6) \times (19 - 24) \times (0.35 + 0.15)$ (2)

8 How far short of 2 hours is 4,978 seconds? Express your answer in seconds. (4)

Across:

10 Green stickers are priced at 10p each and red stickers at 35p each. Kevin bought eight green stickers and two red stickers. How much did he pay, in pence, on average per sticker? (2)

11 $(2 \times 3 \times 4 \times 13)/(2 + 3 + 4 + 3)$ (2)

12 A number, Y, is added to sixteen and the result is multiplied by twenty to give three thousand one hundred and sixty. What is the value of Y? (3)

14 $(24{,}500 \div 500) - 27$ (2)

Down:

10 Take the smallest even number of those below away from the largest even number and divide the result by the sum of the two smallest numbers. (4)

13 10,000 millilitres of water is in a container. 20 litres of water is added to this container. If 80% of the water then is drunk, how many litres is this? (2)

14 Anya made six tubs of ice cream. It cost her £5.60 to make the ice cream. She sold each tub for 98p. How much profit did she make, in pence? (2)

Working out:

Crossword 4: Number Value

Across:

2   2.25 million divided by one thousand. (4)

5   Round 13.71 to one decimal place and then multiply the answer by 10. (3)

6   Multiply 19 by 10. (3)

7   Round 575 to the nearest 10. (3)

9   How many hundreds of thousands are equivalent to 28,100,000? (3)

11 How many times would you need to add 0.02 to −1 to reach 4? (3)

12 Lucy saves 1 pence on three fifths of the days in a non leap year. At the end of the year she divides her total by 10 and rounds the answer to the nearest whole number. What should her answer be in pence? (2)

15 Multiply 0.04699 by 1000 and then round the answer to one decimal place. Give the whole number part of your answer only. (2)

Down:

1   Round 7,824.6 to the nearest whole number. (4)

2   2,910,000 divided by 1000. (4)

3   What is the number value for the digit 5 in the number 23,597? (3)

4   $12,600 \div 200$ (2)

5   Round 1.876 to the nearest hundredth and then multiply the answer by one hundred. (3)

8   How many hundreds are equivalent to 800 tens? (2)

9   Round 204.49 to the nearest whole number. (3)

10 $12,000 \times 100 \div 10 \div 10,000$ (2)

13 Which one of the following numbers does not equal 2,100 when rounded to the nearest 100? (4)

2,149	2,050
2,099	2,049

Across:

17 Kai wrote down the three numbers on the cards below. He then calculated the product of the numbers in the tenths columns. What answer should he have got? (3)

Card 1   Card 2   Card 3

53.21   4.84   0.93

19 What is the number value for the digit 7 in the number 170,430? (5)

Down:

14 Round 145.04781 to the nearest thousandth and then add 1.952 to the result. (3)

16 789 rounded to the nearest 10. (3)

18 What number when multiplied by 30, gives 2,700? (2)

Working out:

Crossword 5: Factor and Multiples

Across:

1 Total number of factors of 80. (2)

2 Ninth multiple of 17. (3)

4 Sum of all the factors of 26. (2)

8 Highest common factor of 260 and 390. (3)

9 Multiple of 11 that is greater than 114 and less than 130. (3)

11 In the incomplete Venn diagram below, what is the highest number that should be entered in the shared area? (2)

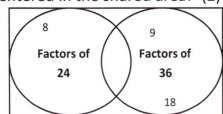

12 Prime factorisation of a number N reveals prime factors of 2, 2 and 5. What is N? (2)

13 If the 4th multiple of N is 36, what is the sum of the first two multiples of N? (2)

14 The first four multiples of a number are 38, N, 114 and 152. What is multiple N? (2)

Down:

1 A number between 11 and 16 that divides exactly into 104. (2)

3 Sum of the first three multiples of 9. (2)

5 Lowest common multiple of 6 and 8. (2)

6 Third multiple of 23 divided by the highest common factor of 9 and 12. (2)

7 Third highest factor of 96. (2)

8 Subtract 100 from the 100th multiple of 13. (4)

9 I am a two-digit number less than 62. I am also a multiple of both 12 and 16. How many factors do I have? (2)

10 A four-digit combination lock code is the first four common factors of 12 and 18 in ascending order. What is the lock number code? (4)

12 What is the sum of the composite numbers in the list below? (4)

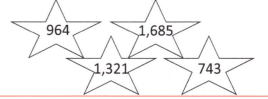

Across:

15 One of the factor pairs of a number *N* is 5 and 7. What is the third multiple of *N*? (3)

17 The result of subtracting the lowest common multiple of 10 and 12 from 323. (3)

19 The result of subtracting the sum of the prime factors of 15 from 6,112. (4)

20 Ten times the sum of all the factors of 66. (4)

Down:

15 The result of squaring the highest common factor of 28 and 42. (3)

16 Add 104 to the eighth multiple of 52. (3)

17 Three of the four factors of *N* are 1, 3 and 17 and the sum of all four factors is 72. What is the 4th multiple of *N*? (3)

18 Lowest common multiple of 5 and 4 multiplied by the highest common factor of 30 and 45. (3)

Working out:

Crossword 6: Number Sequences

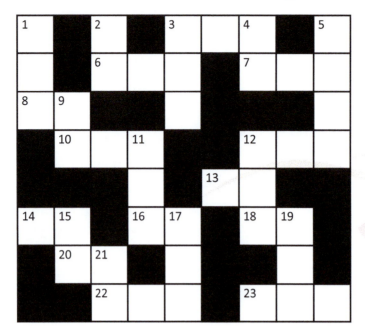

Across:

3   26, 52, 78, 104, 130, ? (3)

6   –1, 3, –9, 27, –81, ? (3)

7   The following set of lengths make up a number sequence:

   30.25km, 60,500m, 12,100,000cm, 242km

   What is the next term in the sequence, in km? (3)

8   What is the sum of the next two terms in the number sequence? (2)

   3, 0, 7, 10, 12, 20

10 What is the missing value in the number sequence? (3)

   0.0422, 4.22, ?, 42,200

12 $115\,^2/_3$, 117, $118\,^1/_3$, $119\,^2/_3$, ? (3)

13 21, 28, 36, 45, ? (2)

14 What is the sum of the next two terms in the number sequence? (2)

   117, 5, 104, 7, 91, 9

16 85, 78, 71, 64, ? (2)

Down:

1   16,896, 4224, 1056, ? (3)

2   A Roman numeral number sequence is shown below. What is the number value of the next term? (2)

   CXII, XCII, LXXII, LII

3   What is the first term in the sequence? (3)

   ?, 135.75, 133.5, 131.25, 129

4   16, 25, 36, 49, ? (2)

5   2,453, 2,437, 2,423, 2,411, ? (4)

9   What is the difference between the next two terms in the number sequence? (2)

   190, 28, 192, 56, 194, 84, ?

11 The first five terms of a number sequence are shown on the chart. What is the sum of the first seven terms of the sequence? (3)

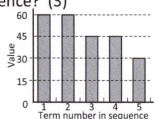

Across:

18 What is the value of the first term in the sequence? (2)

?, 100, 121, 144, 169

20 What is the next term in this sequence? Give your answer in seconds. (2)

7.2 minutes, 2.4 minutes, 0.8 minutes

22 The first 4 terms of a number sequence are as follows. What is the next term? (3)

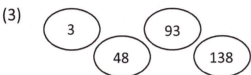

23 What is the next term in the sequence, in pounds(£)? (3)

4p, 20p, £1, £5, £25

Down:

12 34,128, 5,688, 948, ? (3)

15 7, 28, 49, 70, ? (2)

17 What is the first term in the number sequence? (3)

?, 669, 565, 461, 357

19 −123, −60, 3, 66, 129, ? (3)

21 0.061, 0.61, 6.1, ? (2)

Working out:

Crossword 7: Decimal Numbers

Across:

1   Decrease 73.3 by 9.8 and multiply the result by 10. (3)

3   10,450 multiplied by 0.04. (3)

6   How many times would you need to add 0.01 to 0 to reach 5.5? (3)

9   $0.2 \times 0.01 \times 1,000,000$ (4)

10 342.4 divided by 3.2. (3)

11 Troy ate 0.46 of his sandwich at 11am. He then ate two thirds of what remained of his sandwich at noon. What percentage of his sandwich was left after he had finished eating? (2)

12 Pamesh bought three toothbrushes priced at £2.29 each. She paid £7 for the items. How much change did she receive, in pence? (2)

13 Derek bought five DVDs, the costs for which are shown in the table. How much did he spend in total on the DVDs, in pounds(£)? (2)

DVD 1	DVD 2	DVD 3	DVD 4	DVD 5
£12.60	£9.76	£11.08	£12.67	£14.89

Down:

1   What is 66cm as a decimal fraction of 1m? Give your answer as a percentage. (2)

2   8×6.5 (2)

3   What number is represented by the two question marks in the problem below? (2)

$$\begin{array}{r} ?\,?\,.\,9\,3 \\ -\quad\ \ 5\,.\,2\,1 \\ \hline 4\,1\,.\,7\,2 \end{array}$$

4   Add 0.36 to 0.49 and multiply the result by 100. (2)

5   Round the smallest decimal number in the set below to the nearest whole number. (4)

4,067.67, 4,067.7, 4,067.007, 4,077.07

7   $754.13 + 448.87$ (4)

8   $6,352.642 - (-1,663.358)$ (4)

10 How many degrees are equivalent to the sum of the number of degrees in 2.1 right angles? (3)

Across:

15 How many minutes are in 1.65 hours? (2)

18 Take 4.7 from 9.1 and multiply the result by 20. (2)

19 722 × 2.5   (4)

20 How many times greater is 5.75 than 0.25? (2)

Down:

14 What is the result of dividing 1 by 8 and then multiplying the answer by 1000? (3)

16 Calculate the answer to the following problem and then write down the numbers after the decimal point. (3)

2.847 + 1.136

17 61.2/3.4 (2)

Working out:

Crossword 8: Special Numbers

Across:

2 How many short of 7,040 is the sum of the first four square numbers? (4)

5 Four cubed plus seven squared plus eight. (3)

6 Three consecutive whole numbers sum up to 309. What is the smallest of the three numbers? (3)

7 What is the result of multiplying the tenth triangular number by 10? (3)

9 What is the sum of the first six cube numbers? (3)

11 Which value below is closest to 1000? (3)

| 9 squared × 10 | Nine cubed | Roman numeral: CMLIII |

12 What is the sum of Roman numerals XXIV and XXVII? (2)

15 $\sqrt{121} + 4^3 - \sqrt{49}$ (2)

17 How many °C above −13°C is 115°C? (3)

Down:

1 The value of Roman numeral MDV. (4)

2 What is the result of multiplying 514 by the fifth triangular number? (4)

3 What is the difference between the 5th cube number and the sixth prime number? (3)

4 $15 + \sqrt{400} + 90$ (2)

5 What is the result of multiplying the largest prime number less than 20 by $\sqrt{36}$? (3)

8 How many °C below 15°C is −38°C? (2)

9 What is the average of 232 and 73? (3)

10 What is the result of dividing the square root of 225 by the first triangular number? (2)

13 $102 \times \sqrt{144}$ (4)

14 What prime number is between 180 and 190? (3)

Across:

19 The ninth triangular number multiplied by the prime number between 20 and 25 multiplied by √100. (5)

Down:

16 Two identical circles are shown below. What is the diameter of one circle, in mm? (3)

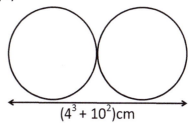

$(4^3 + 10^2)$cm

18 Increase the third cube number by the third triangular number. (2)

Working out:

Crossword 9: Number Machines

Across:

1   The output of the number machine below. (2)

     Input = 8 → [x 12] → Output

2   The input to the number machine below. (4)

     Input → [÷ 5] → [– 421] → Output = 144

6   A number machine adds 87 to its input and multiplies the result by 4. It then subtracts 19 from the result to get the output. The input is 10. What is the output? (3)

7   What number is represented by the question mark in the number machine below? (3)

     Input = 218 → [– ?] → [x √16] → Output = 12^2

9   The output of the number machine below. (2)

     Input = 0.4 → [x 17] → [+ 4.2] → Output

Down:

1   A number machine divides its input by 2 and adds 18 to the result to get the output. The output is 64. What is the input? (2)

3   The output of the number machine below. (2)

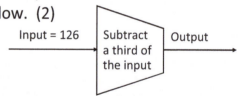

     Input = 126 → [Subtract a third of the input] → Output

4   The output of the number machine below, if n = 6. (3)

     Input = n → [÷ 0.1] → [+ n] → [x 8] → Output

5   The input to the number machine below. (2)

     Input → [+ $\frac{17}{4}$] → [÷ 67] → Output = $\frac{3}{4}$

Across:

10 The input to the number machine below. (2)

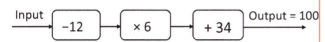

11 The output of the money number machine below, in pence. (2)

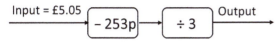

12 A number machine multiplies its input by 8 and adds 51 to the result to get the output. The input is 7. What is the output? (3)

14 A time number machine is shown below. The time on the clock face is the input to the number machine and it shows the time one morning. How many minutes after 8am is the output time? (2)

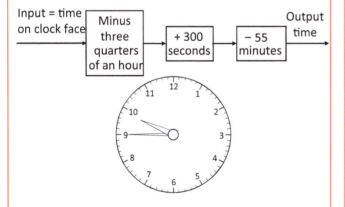

Down:

6 The output of the number machine below. (4)

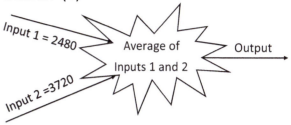

7 The output of the Roman numeral number machine below, in number format. (2)

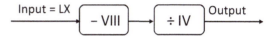

8 A number machine subtracts 300 from its input and divides the result by 200 to get the output. The output is 11. What is the input? (4)

10 The output of the number machine below, in grams. (4)

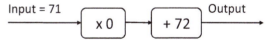

13 The output of the number machine below. (2)

14 What number is represented by the question mark in the number machine below? (2)

Crossword 10: Algebra

1			2	3			4	5
6					7		
8				9		10	
11			12		13	
		14				
15		16			17		18
	19			20		

Across:

1. If $x \div 8 = 7$, what is the value of x? (2)

2. Work out $7s - 3t$, if $s = 45$ and $t = 12$. (3)

4. Omar thinks of a number x and doubles it. He then adds 9 and gets a final answer of 37. Work out the value of x. (2)

8. Solve the equation to find p,

   $2p + \sqrt{9} = 385$. (3)

9. There are 464 green and blue counters in a box. There are three times as many green counters as blue counters. How many green counters are in the box? (3)

11. Using the equation, $y = 5x - 2$, work out the missing value N in the table below. (2)

x	4	5	8
y	18	N	38

12. Solve the equation to find c,

   $338 \div c = 13$. (2)

Down:

1. If $b + 12 = 63$, what is the value of b? (2)

3. Solve the equation to find y,

   $4y = 288$. (2)

5. Work out $5(c^2 + d)$, if $c = 2$ and $d = 4$. (2)

6. If $r = 57$, what is the value of s in the equation, $2r \div 3s = 2$? (2)

7. A number is halved and seven taken away from the result. If the final answer is five, what was the original number? (2)

8. Solve the equation to find b,

   $5b = 3b + 2612$. (4)

9. Solve the equation to find x,

   $2x - 15 = 57$. (2)

10. If $s = 29$ and $t = 1$, evaluate

   $10(s + t)(s - t)$. (4)

12. What is the value of k in the equation

   $6k + 1,900 = 9k - 6,200$? (4)

Across:

13 If s is doubled and t is halved in the equation $s/t = 12$, what will be the new answer? (2)

14 Kim is one third of her father's age. Three years ago Kim was 7. How old was Kim's father three years ago? (2)

15 Work out $9b/8c$ if $b = 72$ and $c = 0.5$. (3)

17 If $y = 0$ work out the value of x in the equation $3x - 315 = 4y$. (3)

19 If $s = 4$, solve this equation to find s, $(60 + 40)/s$. (2)

20 The three sides of a triangle have lengths of $3x$, $4x$ and $6x$. If its perimeter is 26cm, what is the length of the longest side, in cm? (2)

Down:

15 The perimeter of the rectangle below is 30cm. What is the combined length of its two longest sides, in cm? (2)

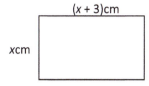

16 If $3(r - 2) = 840$, what is the value of r? (3)

17 Find the value of k in the equation,

$k = 528 - 3k$. (3)

18 I am p years of age, my brother's age is $p + 5$ and my sister's age is $p - 2$. If our combined ages are 153 years, how old am I? (2)

Working out:

Crossword 11: Fractions and Mixed Numbers

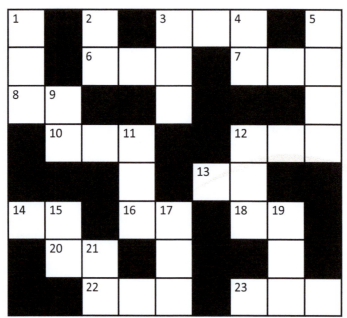

Across:

3   $(^1/_3 + {}^2/_5) \times 225$ (3)

6   Delma gave two thirds of the money she had to Frank. She gave £3.46 to Frank. How much money, in pence, did Delma have originally? (3)

7   What is three quarters of three hundred and sixty-four? (3)

8   How many fifths is $10\,^4/_5$? (2)

10 What is seven tenths multiplied by the sum of the interior angles in a square? (3)

12 Convert $^{11}/_{50}$ into a decimal and multiply the result by 2,000. (3)

13 Sonia has two circles. The diameter of the first circle is two fifths the diameter of the second circle. The diameter of the second circle is 16cm. What is the radius of the first circle in mm? (2)

14 $^2/_3$ of 69. (2)

16 $^7/_8$ of 56 pence. (2)

Down:

1   A rugby team played 360 games in a ten year period. They won $^3/_8$ and drew $^1/_4$ of their games. They lost the remainder. How many games did they lose? (3)

2   John found the difference between the largest and smallest fractions below. He then multiplied the result by 30. What answer should he have got? (2)

$$^3/_5 \quad ^1/_3 \quad ^5/_6 \quad ^1/_2 \quad ^3/_4$$

3   What is $^1/_6$ of 11.4 metres in centimetres? (3)

4   Reduce $^{81}/_{156}$ to its lowest terms and give the denominator of the result. (2)

5   What is eleven twelfths of an hour? Give the answer in seconds. (4)

9   $21\,^3/_4 + 25\,^3/_4 - 5\,^1/_2$ (2)

11 What is the value of the question mark below? (3)

$$\frac{7}{9} = \frac{?}{288}$$

12 What is a seventh of 2,947? (3)

Across:

18 How many more circles in the diagram below need to be coloured black to make the fraction of black circles equal to six tenths? (2)

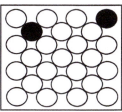

20 $319 \times {}^2/_{11}$ (2)

22 $18\,{}^1/_2 \div {}^1/_8$ (3)

23 $({}^1/_2 + {}^1/_3) \times 600$ (3)

Down:

15 Bolin converts $10\,{}^5/_6$ into an improper fraction. What should the numerator be? (2)

17 Subtract ${}^3/_5$ of 20 from 1000. (3)

19 A chef made 585 pancakes. One third of the pancakes had orange juice on them and the rest had lemon juice. How many pancakes had lemon juice on them? (3)

21 What is the result of the problem below? (2)

$${}^9/_2 \times 18$$

Working out:

Crossword 12: Percentages

```
 1       2        3       4        5
                        6
    7       8
    9               10
                11
12       13  14      15  16
    17          18
    19          20
```

Across:

1   Of all the pages in a 290-page magazine, 50% have no twelve-letter words, 20% have one, 20% have two and the remaining pages have three twelve-letter words, respectively. How many twelve-letter words are in the magazine? (3)

3   100% of 733. (3)

6   What is 15% of four tonnes in kilograms? (3)

9   400% of 1872. (4)

10 A park has 700 trees. 58% are sycamore trees, how many is this? (3)

11 What is twelve hours out of five days as a percentage? (2)

12 What is £5.88 as a percentage of £16.80? (2)

13 20% of 180. (2)

15 Consider a square. What is the length of one side as a percentage of its perimeter? (2)

Down:

1   If six pupils represent 25% of the pupils in a class, how many pupils are in the class? (2)

2   10% of 120. (2)

3   What is 0.71 as a percentage? (2)

4   Olivia saw a toaster for sale at £30, but she forgot to add on VAT at 20%. What was the total price of the toaster in pounds(£)? (2)

5   98% of 5,200. (4)

7   65% of 4,300. (4)

8   4,580 people were asked what their favourite colour was. However, 15% of those asked did not respond. How many did respond? (4)

10 What is 20% of £20.10, in pence? (3)

14 A computer normally sells for £680, but is reduced in price by 5%. What is its new price, in pounds(£)? (3)

16 Lee adds 26% of 300 to 500. What result should he get? (3)

Across:

18 What percentage of the circle below is shaded? (2)

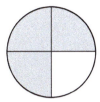

19 What is 114% of 900? (4)

20 What is 2.8 minutes out of 10 minutes, as a percentage? (2)

Down:

17 What is the size of angle *X* as a percentage of the sum of the interior angles in the triangle? (2)

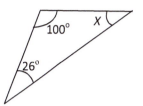

Working out:

Crossword 13: Ratio

Across:

2 15.225 litres of water is shared between Brian and Ayesha in the ratio 4:1. How much water will Ayesha receive, in millilitres? (4)

5 Maria has 330 stickers. For every 29 square stickers there is one circular sticker. How many circular stickers does she have? (2)

6 £14.40 was split between Isabella, Sophie and Simon in the ratio 2:7:3. How much did Sophie receive in pence? (3)

7 For every 30 minutes Arnaud worked at his computer he got up and exercised for 150 seconds. If he exercised for 55 minutes, how many minutes did he work for? (3)

9 In a supermarket, 3 in every 5 people were wearing jeans. There were 315 people in the supermarket, how many were wearing jeans? (3)

11 What number does n equal below? (3)

$$14:29 = n:319$$

Down:

1 For every £300.75 Lucy makes at work, she gives her daughter £38.50. If she gives her daughter £308, how much money had Lucy made at work, in pounds(£)? (4)

2 A box contains 10p and 50p coins in the ratio 7:3. There are forty-two 50p coins. How much money is in the box, in pence? (4)

3 What number does n equal below? (3)

$$27:40 = 324:n$$

4 On a school trip the ratio of adults to children was 3:13. If twenty-one adults went on the trip, how many children went? (2)

5 The ratio of lorries to cars is 2:9. There are 162 cars. How many lorries and cars are there in total? (3)

8 Barbara and Katy have several 10.5g coins. For every five coins Katy has, Barbara has two. If Katy has fifteen coins, how much in total (in grams) do Barbara's coins weigh? (2)

Across:

12 Jade cuts a 28cm bread stick in the ratio 6:1. What is the length of the shorter part, in mm? (2)

13 Work has begun on shading a number of tiles on the grid below. Once finished, for every one tile unshaded there will be three tiles shaded. How many more tiles will need to be shaded in total? (2)

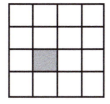

15 In a school, the ratio of girls to boys is 5:4 and there are 1,062 pupils. How many more girls than boys are there? (3)

Down:

9 There are 846 marbles in a box. They are either green or pink and are in the ratio 1:5. How many green marbles are there? (3)

11 Chirag had 70 sweets. He split the sweets in the ratio 3:2:2 between himself, his sister and his brother. How many more sweets did Chirag have than his brother? (2)

12 A team won 96 medals at the Olympics. The ratio of gold to silver to bronze medals won was 1:2:3. How many bronze medals did the team win? (2)

14 A row of shapes has the following repeating pattern. How many circles will there be if there are 20 triangles? (2)

Working out:

Crossword 14: Representing Data

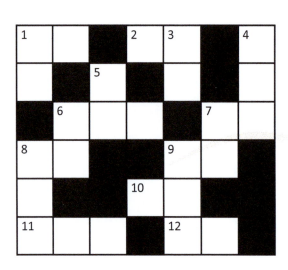

Across:

1   The frequency table below shows the results of a survey that asked people which types of butterfly they had seen recently. How many people had seen a Grayling? (2)

Butterfly Type	Tally	Frequency
No Butterfly	＋＋＋ ＋＋＋ ＋＋＋ III	18
Brimstone	＋＋＋ IIII	9
Grayling	＋＋＋ ＋＋＋ ＋＋＋	?
Swallowtail	＋＋＋ ＋＋＋ I	11

2   Ticket sales for a concert are shown on the line graph. How many hundreds of tickets were sold on the fifth day? (2)

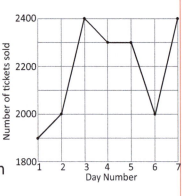

6   Sapna bought two of everything on the list. How much did she pay in total, in pounds(£)? (3)

Item	Cost per item
Clock	£11.55
Printer	£62.50
Scanner	£46.75
Lamp	£9.70

Down:

1   This chart shows the lengths of six songs. How many seconds over three and a half minutes is the longest song? (2)

3   A group of people were asked if they had read a book (B) or magazine (M) in the last month. The results are shown in the Venn diagram. How many people had read a magazine? (2)

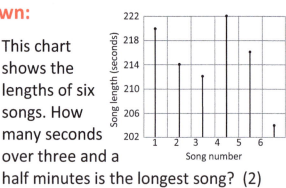

4   1,600 people were asked what their favourite dance was. The results are shown in the pie chart below. How many people said Salsa was their favourite? (3)

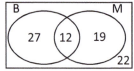

Across:

7. This chart shows the results of a survey that asked people about their eye colours. Of the people surveyed, how many did not have blue eyes? (2)

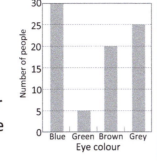

8. The prices of some food items are shown below. How much would forty cakes, sixteen bottles of water and four sandwiches cost in pounds (£)? (2)

5 cakes	£9.20
8 bottles of water	£6.40
4 sandwiches	£7.60

9. The highest temperatures on five days were recorded and shown on this chart. What was the average daily highest temperature in °C? (2)

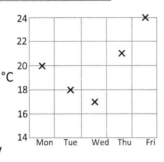

10. Using the same chart as in clue 9 above, how many °C below 40°C was the temperature on Tuesday? (2)

11. The weights of five boxes are shown on the chart below. What is the combined weight (in grams) of boxes 2, 4 and 5? (3)

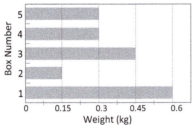

12. Using the same chart as in clue 11 above, what is the result (in grams) of subtracting the median box weight from 358g? (2)

Down:

5. Calculate the average speed in miles per hour from the line graph below. (2)

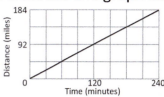

6. The following table shows the number of houses for sale in an area. How many houses have two or more bedrooms and a garden? (2)

No. of houses available	No. of bedrooms	Garage	Garden
13	5	No	Yes
11	2	Yes	Yes
9	3	Yes	No
7	1	No	Yes
12	4	Yes	No

7. Thirty two children were asked about their favourite fruit juice. The results are in the table. What percentage of the children were boys? (2)

	Fruit juice flavour		
	Orange	Apple	Mango
Boys	9	4	3
Girls	5	7	4

8. In total how many bikes were sold on days 2, 3 and 4? (3)

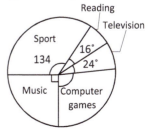

9. Andrea spent 675 minutes on the following activities. How many minutes did she spend on television and computer games? (3)

Crossword 15: Mean, Median, Mode and Range

Across:

1   Mean of 22, 38, 89, 25 and 71. (2)

2   Range of 26, 239, 338, 28, 216 and 335. (3)

4   Median of 18, 48, 25, 9, 32, 41 and 33. (2)

8   Mode of 448, 443, 448, 446, 443, 448, 446, 443, 446 and 448. (3)

9   Range of weights listed below, in kg. (3)

Weight kg	104	57	378	256	47	59	369

11 The scores from throwing a die six times are 4, 1, 4, 4, 5 and 6. What is the product of the mean and mode scores? (2)

12 Median of 17, 31, 24.5, 18, 33 and 27.5. (2)

13 The sum of two positive whole numbers is 81 and the range is 5. What is the smaller of the two numbers? (2)

14 Mode of 58, 62, 63, 58, 62, 62, 58 and 62. (2)

Down:

1   Mode of 48, 43, 48, 46, 43, 46, 43 and 49. (2)

3   Median of 13, 17, 9, 22, 7 and 15. (2)

5   Average of the ages below, in years. (2)

Age in years	26	17	31	25	19	26

6   Range of 18, −8, 41, −4, 46, 38 and 44. (2)

7   Median of the five prices below, in pence. (2)

£1.24, £0.82, £0.67, £1.12 and £0.93

8   Sophie's last four computer game scores were 4632, 4218, 4741 and 4825. What was her mean score? (4)

9   What must be the missing number N in the set below for the mode to be 36? (2)

34, 36, 33, 31, 36, 34, N

10 The heights of four mountains in Scotland are hm, 1,309m, 1,214m and 1,221m. If their mean height is 1,272m, what is h, in metres? (4)

Across:

15 The mean of 11 numbers is 22. What must be the sum of the 11 numbers? (3)

17 A small plane travels 365 miles in 2 ½ hours. What is the average speed of the plane in miles per hour(mph)? (3)

19 What is the range of the number set below if the sum of all the numbers is 69? (2)

$$\textcircled{15} \quad \textcircled{11} \quad \textcircled{7} \quad \textcircled{17} \quad \textcircled{?}$$

20 What is the sum of the mean, median, mode and range of the set of numbers below? (2)

4, 2, 5, 5, 4 and 4

Down:

12 Range of 71, 2335, 57, 2333 and 2336. (4)

15 Three of the numbers in a set of five numbers are 6, 9 and 4. If the mode for the set is 2, what is the sum of the set? (2)

16 Median of 0.29kg, 0.12kg, 0.262kg, 0.08kg, 0.14kg and 0.283kg expressed in grams. (3)

17 For the number set below, what is the product of the range and median? (3)

5, 12, 18, 7, 3

18 Average of the test marks shown below. (2)

Test Marks	59	68	64	59	60	68

Working out:

Crossword 16: Probability

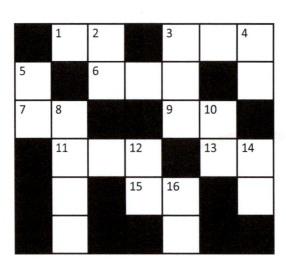

Across:

1   Thirty pages in a book have pictures and 220 pages have no pictures. A page is chosen at random, what is the probability, as a percentage, it has a picture? (2)

3   A fair die is thrown 501 times. How many times would you expect the die to land on a 3 or 5? (3)

6   The spinner below is spun 624 times. How many times would you expect it to land on a triangular number? (3)

7   Adil has 600 coins. Thirty-seven are 5p, eleven are 10p, thirty-one are 20p, fifteen are 50p, twenty are £1 and the rest are £2. If he selects a coin at random, what is the probability, as a percentage, he will select a £2 coin? (2)

Down:

2   Janet throws a fair die and a fair coin. What is the probability, as a percentage, that the die lands on an even number and the coin lands heads up? (2)

3   The probability of rain on any given day is $^1/_5$. How many days would you expect it to rain in the next 515 days? (3)

4   A bag contains marbles. Five are purple, six are blue, three are yellow and 6 are orange. A marble is selected at random. What is the probability, as a percentage, that it is not purple? (2)

5   The probability a squash player wins a game is $^{14}/_{25}$. If he plays 175 games, how many is he likely to win? (2)

8   A drawer contains paper clips. 60% are metal and the rest are plastic. If 2,860 paper clips are removed at random, how many would you expect to be made of plastic? (4)

Across:

9   An office has 200 rulers. Seventy six are 30cm and the rest are 15cm. If one is selected randomly, what is the probability, as a percentage, it is 30cm in length? (2)

11   A firm makes lamps. If the probability that any lamp is faulty is 10%, how many lamps out of 1,930 are likely to be faulty? (3)

13   The ace of hearts and three of diamonds are removed from a standard pack of 52 playing cards. Of the cards that remain, what is the probability, as a percentage, of selecting a card with a value between 2 and 8? (2)

15   On a history test, twelve pupils scored less than 10, twenty-one scored between 10 and 19 and twenty-seven scored between 20 and 30. What is the probability, as a percentage, that a pupil selected at random scored less than 20? (2)

Down:

10   A tile is selected at random from the grid below. What is the probability, as a percentage, that the tile does not contain a quadrilateral? (2)

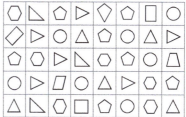

12   Using the grid in clue 10 above, a tile is selected. What is the probability, as a percentage, that it contains a triangle? (2)

14   A letter is chosen from those which make up the word below. What is the probability, as a percentage, that the letter is a L or O? (2)

L I K E L I H O O D

16   A fair die is thrown. What is the probability of it landing on an even number, as a percentage? (2)

Working out:

Crossword 17: Reading Scales

Across:

1   By how many millimetres is the reading on the ruler less than 4.9cm? (2)

2   A large map is produced with a scale of 1:12,500. What distance on the map in millimetres, represents 32.65km in reality? (4)

6   How many more kilograms would need to be added to the weight shown below to make 7.392 tonnes? (3)

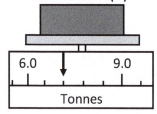

7   What is the result of subtracting the length of the diameter of the circle below from 265mm? Give your answer in mm. (3)

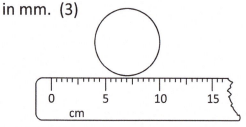

Down:

1   What is the average temperature on the thermometers shown? (2)

3   What reading is shown on the petrol gauge below, in litres? The reading is exactly halfway between the nearest two divisions. (2)

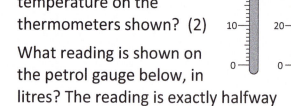

4   How many 5ml spoons could be filled from all the liquid in the jug? (3)

5   A diagram of a building is drawn in the scale of 1cm to 2.6m. The building is 15cm high on the drawing. How high is the building in reality in metres? (2)

Across:

9 How many degrees (°C) above minus 25°C is the temperature displayed ? (2)

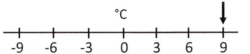

10 A scale is shown below in metres. What is the distance between the two measurements, in centimetres? (2)

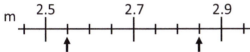

11 What is the perimeter of the regular polygon below, in millimetres? (2)

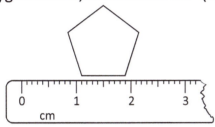

12 Bokang placed some potatoes on the scale at her local shop. How much did the potatoes cost, in pence, if the price was £1.10 per kilogram? (3)

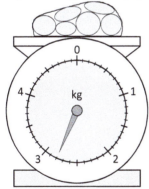

14 A map is produced with a scale of 1:700. What distance, in metres, would be represented by 10cm on the map? (2)

Down:

6 Measurement on the scales, in grams. (4)

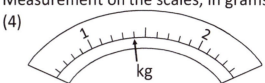

7 A map is produced with a scale of 1:3600. What distance on the map, in centimetres, would represent 720m in reality? (2)

8 Two identical objects A and B are shown on the scales below. How much does object B weigh, in grams? (4)

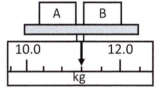

10 How many more millilitres would need to be added to the container below to fill it to its 6 litre capacity? (4)

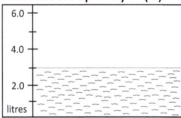

13 Using the diagram in clue 10 above, what is 2.8% of the water level shown? Give answer in millilitres. (2)

14 Increase the temperature on the thermometer by 48°C. (2)

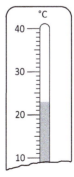

Crossword 18: Length, Weight and Capacity

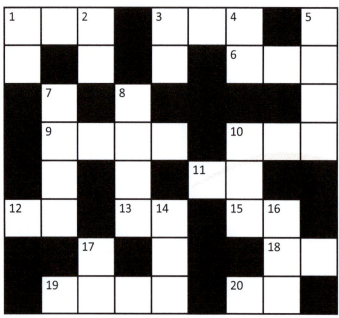

Across:

1 10.2cm in mm. (3)

3 What is the sum of 0.341 tonnes and 420,000 grams, in kilograms? (3)

6 What is the difference between 26,000mm and 0.82km, in metres? (3)

9 If 1 stone = 14 pounds and 1 pound = 16 ounces, how many ounces are there in 5.5 stone? (4)

10 One bottle holds 1.8 litres of water and a second bottle holds 70% of this amount. What is the difference, in millilitres, of water between the bottles? (3)

11 Rocky is 5 feet 10 inches tall. How many inches is this short of 82 inches? Use the fact that 1 foot = 12 inches. (2)

12 If £1 = €1.2 Euros, how many Euros is 2000 pence? (2)

13 If 1 gallon ≈ 4 litres, approximately how many gallons is 76,000 millilitres? (2)

Down:

1 A container holds 3.63 litres of water. How many 330ml cans could be filled using all the water? (2)

2 28,000 grams in kilograms. (2)

3 If a bottle holding 1.75 litres of water is emptied and its contents fill exactly 25 small cups, what is the capacity of each cup in millilitres? (2)

4 If a £2 coin roughly weighs 12 grams, how many £2 coins are the equivalent of 204 grams? (2)

5 If 1 mile = 1,760 yards and 1 mile ≈ 2km, how many yards are in 5km? (4)

7 A tree is 781cm high. A tree surgeon removes 2/5 the tree's height. How much did he cut down, in mm? (4)

8 What is the sum of the weights of parcels 1 and 2 below, in grams? (4)

Across:

15 What is the average weight below, in kg? **(2)**

69000g   75kg   60kg

18 The combined weight of six identical boxes is 0.438 tonnes. How much does one box weigh, in kilograms? **(2)**

19 1.27kg in grams. **(4)**

20 If 1 pint ≈ 600 millilitres, how many pints of water are in the beaker approximately? **(2)**

9 litres of water

Down:

10 Lily has a 4.126 litre container full of water. The container has a leak where 0.6 litres of water is lost every ninety seconds. How many millilitres of water will be left in the container after nine minutes? **(3)**

14 0.0094km in cm. **(3)**

16 If 1oz ≈ 25g, what is 35oz approximately in grams? **(3)**

17 The perimeter of a square is 56 yards. If 1 yard = 3 feet, what is a single side length of the square, in feet? **(2)**

Working out:

Crossword 19: Dates, Time and Timetables

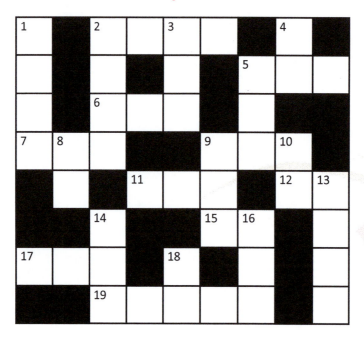

Across:

2 What time is 10.18pm in 24 hour clock format, written as HHMM? (4)

5 How many seconds are in 5.75 minutes? (3)

6 A train leaves Bournemouth station at 11.57am and calls at the following stations on its way to Waterloo. A passenger on board plays a number of 10-second games. How many games could the passenger play between Bournemouth and Woking? (3)

Station	Arrival times
Brockenhurst	12:14
Southampton	12:31
Winchester	12:47
Woking	13:19
Waterloo	13:49

7 13.75 minutes in seconds. (3)

9 Using the timetable in clue 6 above, if there was a delay on route and the train arrived at Waterloo 69 minutes late, how long was the journey from Bournemouth, in minutes? (3)

Down:

1 1.1 days + 5.3 hours + 960 seconds, in minutes. (4)

2 What is quarter to nine in the evening in 24 hour clock format, written as HHMM? (4)

3 How many days in total are in June, July, August and September? (3)

4 Tara has exams on 6th March and 8th April. Inclusive of these dates, how many days are between the dates? (2)

5 How many minutes are between 03:53 and 10:11 the same morning? (3)

8 Use part of the calendar below to determine the date of the fifth Thursday in November. (2)

9 How many hours are 6,420 minutes? (3)

Across:

11 How many minutes are between the times shown on the clock faces below? Both times are after 12 noon but before midnight on the same day. (3)

12 How many hours are between quarter to five one afternoon and 16:45 the next day? (2)

15 1896 hours in days. (2)

17 1.7 hours in minutes. (3)

19 1000 hours plus 540 seconds, in minutes. (5)

Down:

10 Clock A shows a time of 11.25am and zero seconds and clock B shows a time of 11.28am and zero seconds. Clock B gains 15 seconds every day, while clock A does not gain or lose any time. How many days ago did both clocks show exactly the same time? (2)

13 How many minutes are in 3 days? (4)

14 How many hours are in 5.25 days? (3)

16 How many days are in 2.6 non-leap years? (3)

18 How many hours in total are the mornings of the weekdays during one week? (2)

Working out:

Crossword 20: Lines, Angles and Bearings

	1		2	3			4
5		6				7	
		8	9		10		
	11		12	13		14	15
16				17			
		18				19	
20					21		

Across:

2 What is the smaller angle between 5 and 9 on a clock face? (3)

5 Kim is facing north-east and turns clockwise to face south. How many degrees has Kim turned through? (3)

7 Which one of the following randomly numbered statements is true? (2)

    25: Parallel lines never cross
    55: Perpendicular lines cross at 45°
    38: Parallel lines cross at 60°
    65: Perpendicular lines never cross

8 In the quadrilateral shown below, how many degrees make up the unknown angle *B*? (2)

124° 102° 108° *B*

Down:

1 In the diagram below, what is the result of subtracting the longest vertical line from the longest sloping line, in mm? (2)

2.9cm 4.7cm 4.1cm 9.7cm 4.8cm 3.5cm 5.4cm

3 Ali walks 18m north. He turns and walks 12m east. He turns again and walks 18m south. Finally, he turns and walks 16m east. How far, in metres, is Ali from the point where he started? (2)

4 How many degrees make up angle *A* in the diagram below? (2)

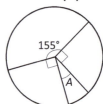
155° *A*

5 One end of a horizontal line has a y-coordinate of 17. What is the y-coordinate halfway along the line? (2)

Across:

10 On the map below Nye is standing northeast of the shop, Kai is standing west of Nye and Jan is standing south of Kai. At which number marked location is Jan standing? (2)

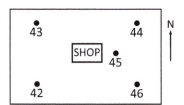

12 The four lines shown below are joined end to end to form the shape of a rectangle. What is the distance around the outside of the shape in cm if line length *n* = 8cm? (2)

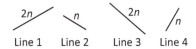

14 Point P is moved 26m west, 18m north, 77m east and lastly 18m south. The resulting point is called Q. What is the shortest distance between the original point P and the resulting point Q, in metres? (2)

16 In the triangle shown below, how many degrees make up the unknown angle *A*? (2)

17 Straight line S has end coordinates of (3, 7) and (9, 7). Straight line T has end coordinates of (3, 3) and (9, 3). Which one of the following four randomly numbered statements is true? (2)

16: S and T are converging
11: S and T are perpendicular
19: S and T are parallel
13: S and T are diverging

Down:

6 In the diagram below, what is angle P, in degrees? (2)

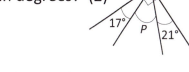

7 What angle in degrees must the wheel below turn through in a clockwise direction for the arrow to point to P? (3)

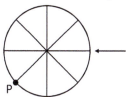

9 One end of a vertical line has an x-coordinate of 64. What is the x-coordinate at the opposite end of the line? (2)

11 Duncan is standing on the black square below. He walks one square north, two squares west, three squares south and one square east. What number square does Duncan finish on? (2)

87	43	17	25	36	14
60	12	29	33	45	71
23	52	59	■	15	68
11	26	13	41	50	18
92	16	72	19	82	94

N ↑

13 The steering wheel of some cars can be turned through two and a quarter revolutions. What is the equivalent of this rotation, in degrees? (3)

Across:

18 Kate is facing southwest. She turns anticlockwise to face northeast. What angle in degrees has Kate turned through? (3)

20 The five angles shown below have each been assigned a random three figure number. Which number relates to an obtuse angle? (3)

163   119   142   138   159

21 How many degrees are equivalent to three and a half right angles? (3)

Down:

15 On the grid of squares below, the numbers marked on the lines are their lengths in cm. What is the total length of the lines with an angle of 45° with the horizontal? (2)

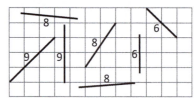

18 Town B is 13km south of town A and town C is 5km north of town B. Town D is 4km north of town A. What is the shortest distance, in km, between town C and town D? (2)

19 Two of the interior angles of a triangle are 105° and 54°. How many degrees make up the third angle? (2)

Working out:

Working out:

Crossword 21: 2D Shapes

Across:

1   How many sides does a decagon have? (2)

2   What is the sum of the number of sides on the shapes below? (2)

6   What is the result of multiplying the number of pairs of parallel sides on a regular hexagon by 24? (2)

8   Each of the terms below has a random number assigned to it. Sum the random numbers that have terms relating to parts of a circle. (3)

> 23: Polygon
> 13: Semicircle
> 18: Sector
> 45: Oblong
> 29: Kite
> 90: Circumference
> 83: Arc
> 68: Quadrilateral
> 11: Radius
> 97: Rhombus

Down:

1   What is the radius of the circle below, in mm? (4)

Diameter = 324.2cm

3   What percentage of the shapes below are quadrilaterals? (2)

4   The three triangles below have random numbers assigned to them. What is the random number associated with the isosceles triangle? (3)

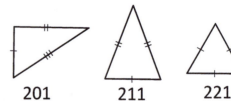

201   211   221

5   What is the sum of the number of corners on a triangle, a heptagon, a nonagon, a parallelogram and a trapezium? (2)

Across:

9 The shapes below have random numbers assigned to them. What number is associated with the parallelogram? (2)

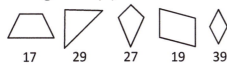

17   29   27   19   39

11 Sum of the interior angles in a hexagon. (3)

14 The shapes listed below have random numbers assigned to them. What number is associated with the shape that looks most like a circle? (3)

       157: Scalene Triangle
       257: Kite
       357: Regular Nonagon
       457: Symmetrical Trapezium
       557: Regular Pentagon
       657: Rectangle

16 Sum of the interior angles in an octagon. (4)

17 The two circles below are concentric. The diameter of the larger circle is 20m. The diameter of the smaller circle is 55% of the diameter of the larger circle. What is the radius of the smaller circle, in cm? (3)

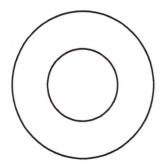

Down:

7 What is the result of multiplying the number of acute angles in an equilateral triangle by 9? (2)

8 In total, how many sides of five regular quadrilaterals are of equal length? (2)

10 Four identical circles are shown below. What is the radius of one of the circles, in cm? (3)

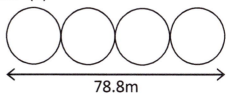

78.8m

12 What is the sum of the number of sides of 200 hexagons, 60 heptagons, 50 octagons and 30 triangles? (4)

13 A regular pentagon is shown below. What is the size of angle X? (3)

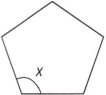

15 What percentage of the shapes below are polygons? (2)

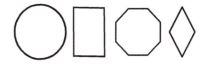

Crossword 22: Perimeter and Area

Across:

1 The perimeter of a square is 1,040mm. What is the length of one of its sides, in cm? (2)

2 What is the area of the garden below, in m^2? (4)

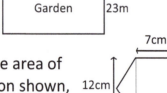

6 What is the area of the hexagon shown, in cm^2? (3)

7 Shape S is shown on a grid of squares below. If each square has a perimeter of 32cm, what is the area of shape S, in cm^2? (3)

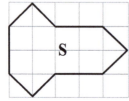

9 How many square tiles with side length 30cm would be needed to cover an oblong of length 2.7m and width 1.5m? (2)

Down:

1 What is the area of the triangle below, in cm^2? (2)

3 A rhombus has a side length of 1,500cm. What is its perimeter, in metres? (2)

4 What is the sum of the perimeters of the shapes below, in mm? (3)

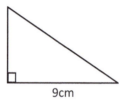

5 What is the perimeter of the shape below, in cm? (2)

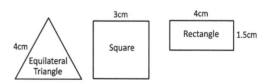

Across:

10 The perimeter of a regular nonagon is 171,000m. What is the length of one of its sides, in km? (2)

11 The perimeter of the rectangle below is 800cm. What is b in cm? (2)

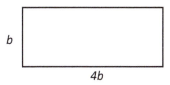

12 Find the area of the base space (B) on the cuboid below, in cm^2. (3)

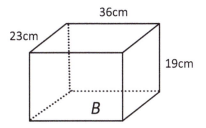

14 Subtract the area of the shape below from 103cm^2. (2)

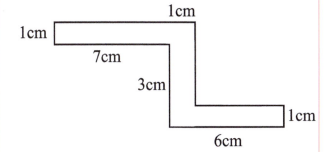

Down:

6 Which of the area values below is closest to the area of London? (4)
   1,872cm^2
   1,074m^2
   1,572km^2

7 The area of a right-angled triangle is 1,580mm^2. Its base length is 4cm, what is its height, in mm? (2)

8 What is the perimeter of the isosceles triangle below, in cm? (4)

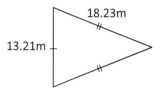

10 The area of a square is 625cm^2. What is its perimeter, in mm? (4)

13 Two identical circles are shown inside a rectangle below. If the radius of each circle is 7cm, what is the perimeter of the rectangle, in cm? (2)

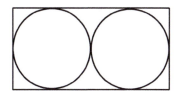

14 A regular pentagon has a side length of Roman numeral XVII centimetres. What is the numerical value for the perimeter of the pentagon, in cm? (2)

Crossword 23: 3D Shapes

Across:

1   How many vertices does a hexagonal prism have? (2)

2   The four shapes below have random numbers underneath them. What random number is associated with the tetrahedron? (4)

2185   2185   2185   2185

6   How many marbles identical to that shown below could fit inside the box? (3)

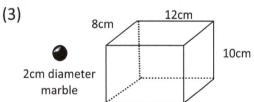

2cm diameter marble

8cm   12cm   10cm

7   What is the result of multiplying the number of faces on the shape below by 34? (3)

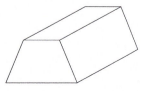

Down:

1   The net below when folded up forms a closed box. What is the height of the box, in mm? (2)

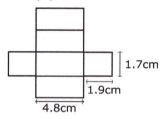

1.7cm
1.9cm
4.8cm

3   How many edges does the shape on the right have? (2)

4   Five nets are shown below with random numbers underneath them. What is the sum of random numbers associated with the nets that form a closed cube when folded up? (3)

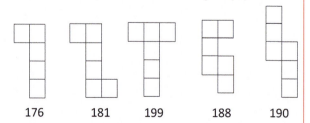

176   181   199   188   190

5   How many edges does a cuboid have? (2)

6   How many faces are on 6 cylinders? (2)

Across:

9 Dawn wants to produce nets for nine identical heptagonal prisms. She has 18 identical heptagons and 15 identical rectangles. How many more rectangles does she need to form the 9 nets? (2)

10 What is the sum of the number of vertices on the shapes below? (2)

11 Akari has 176 identical hemispheres. She glues each one to another one to form spheres. A box can hold 8 spheres. How many boxes can Akari fill? (2)

13 How many faces are on two octahedrons? (2)

15 What is the sum of the number of vertices on the shapes below? (2)

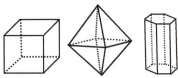

16 What is the sum of all interior angles on all faces of a hexagonal prism? (4)

17 The four shapes below have random numbers underneath them. What random number is associated with the cone? (2)

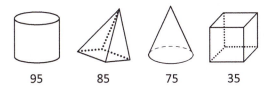

95	85	75	35

Down:

7 What is the result of dividing the number of pairs of parallel faces on an octagonal prism by 0.2? (2)

8 Four shapes are listed below along with a random number. Which random number is associated with the shape that is formed when the net below is folded up? (3)

     401: Square-based pyramid
     476: Tetrahedron
     490: Cone
     456: Triangular prism

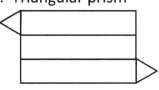

12 How many edges are on 5 octagonal prisms? (3)

13 Four shapes are listed below along with a random number. Which random number is associated with the shape that has twice as many edges as the triangular-based pyramid? (3)

     145: Cone
     187: Hexagonal prism
     135: Cube
     103: Square-based pyramid

14 The net below can be folded to form a cube. Roman numerals are on the faces. What number is on the face which is opposite to the base when the cube is folded up? (2)

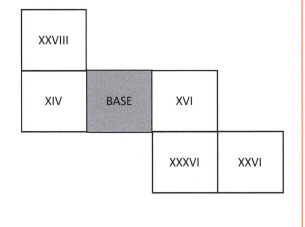

Crossword 24: Volume

Across:

1 The volume of the cuboid below is 728cm^3. What is its length, in cm? (2)

2 The dimensions of a cuboid and a cube are shown below. By how many cm^3 is the volume of the cuboid larger than that of the cube? (4)

> **Cuboid**: length 20cm, width 15cm, height 18cm
> **Cube**: length 12cm

6 The volume of a sphere is 345cm^3 and the volume of a cone is 492cm^3. What is the combined volume of 7 such spheres and 8 such cones, in cm^3? (4)

7 What is the volume of the shape below, in cm^3? (3)

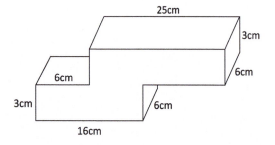

Down:

1 Each cube which makes up the cuboid below has a volume of 52cm^3. What is the volume of the cuboid, in cm^3? (4)

3 The net below makes a cuboid when folded up. The volume of the cuboid is 960cm^3. What is the volume of one of the cubes which makes up the cuboid in cm³? (2)

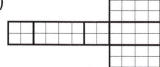

4 A cuboid has length 3m, breadth 10m and height 910cm. What is its volume, in m^3? (3)

5 A cylindrical tin is 24cm in height and the area of its circular base is 66cm^2. What is its volume, in cm^3? (4)

Across:

9   The cuboid shown below has its dimensions expressed in Roman numerals and all values are in millimetres. What is its volume, in cm^3? (2)

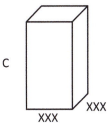

10 The volume of the shape below is 931cm^3. What is the volume of one of the identical cubes in cm^3 that makes up the cuboid? (2)

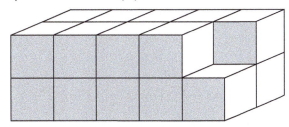

12 The area of a face on a cube is 9cm^2. What is the volume of the cube, in cm^3? (2)

14 Which of the three volume values below is most likely to represent the volume of a toy block? (2)

    76m^3
    17km^3
    64cm^3

15 The volume of a huge cube is 1km^3. What is its height, in m? (4)

16 The volume of the cylinder below is 600cm^3. What is its height, in mm? (3)

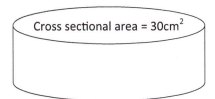

Cross sectional area = 30cm^2

Down:

7   What is the volume of the triangular shaped wedge below, in cm^3? (2)

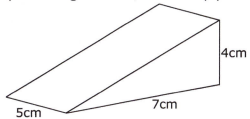

4cm
5cm   7cm

8   A cuboid has length 0.3025m, breadth 4cm and height 70mm. What is its volume, in cm^3? (3)

11 The volume of the hexagonal prism below is given by the area of end B multiplied by its height. The cross section of end B is also shown below as a hexagon. What is the volume of the prism, in cm^3? (3)

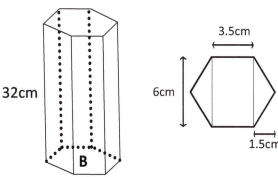

12 The volume of a cube is 125cm^3. What is the perimeter of a face on the cube, in mm? (3)

13 The volume of the cuboid below is 1.8 times the volume of the tetrahedron. What is the breadth(*b*) of the cuboid, in cm? (2)

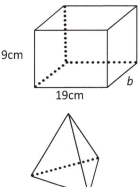

9cm
19cm
b

Volume = 950cm^3

Crossword 25: Co-ordinates

	1		2	3			4
5		6				7	
		8	9		10		
	11		12	13		14	15
16				17			
		18				19	
20					21		

Across:

2 Which one of the following four randomly numbered statements concerning the points on a plotted horizontal line is true? (3)

> 136: One x-coordinate point must be zero
> 124: All y-coordinate points are the same
> 132: All y-coordinate points are different
> 128: All x-coordinate points are the same

5 What is the perimeter of the square below? (3)

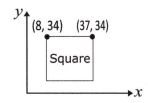

7 The coordinates at the bottom end of a 6-unit long vertical line are (22, 24). What is the y-coordinate at the top end of the line? (2)

8 In the triangle below, the two sides h are the same length. What is the x-coordinate at corner C? (2)

Down:

1 The diagram below shows a 45° line with its bottom end point at coordinates (3, 0) and its top end point at (x, 18). What is the missing x-coordinate value? (2)

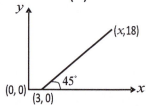

3 A vertical line has end coordinates of (24, 22) and (24, 30). What is the y-coordinate at the centre of the line? (2)

4 What is the x-coordinate at point P on the diagram below? (2)

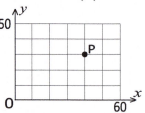

5 What is the distance between two equal length parallel vertical lines L1 and L2 if (3, 5) is a point on L1 and (20, 14) a point on L2? (2)

Across:

10 A horizontal line has a left end x-coordinate value of –19 and a centre x-coordinate value of 6. What is the x-coordinate value at the right end of the line? (2)

12 What is the perimeter of the shape shown below? (2)

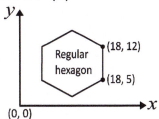

14 The points (2, 5), (10, 5) and (10, 12) are the coordinates of three corners of a rectangle. What is the area of the rectangle? (2)

16 What is the difference between the x-coordinate values at line ends R and P? Point Q is five sixths of the distance along from end P. (2)

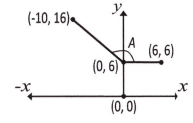

17 What is the distance between two equal length parallel horizontal lines L1 and L2 if (7, 8) is a point on L1 and (12, –4) a point on L2? (2)

18 What is angle *A* in degrees in the diagram below? (3)

Down:

6 What is the x-coordinate on the line below that is one third of the way along from end A? (2)

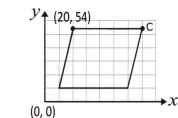

7 Straight line P has end coordinates of (0, 0) and (20, 0). Straight line Q has end coordinates of (0, 0) and (15, 15). What is the larger angle between the two lines in degrees? (3)

9 What is the y-coordinate at corner point C on the parallelogram shown below? (2)

11 The point (3, 2) is at one end of a vertical line. Which one of the following four randomly numbered answers gives two possible coordinates for the other end of the line? (2)

    22: (4, 12) and (4, –6)

    29: (3, 10) and (4, –7)

    25: (2, 15) and (3, 9)

    28: (3, 11) and (3, –8)

13 Adele is standing at point A on the grid below. She walks the route ABCDEF. What distance does Adele walk? (3)

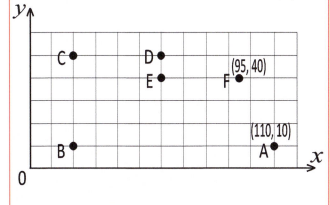

Across:

20 A vertical line L is drawn on graph paper. Which numbered answer below gives two possible end coordinates of a line drawn perpendicular to line L? (3)

       790: (2, 7) and (−9, 7)

       730: (−8, 5) and (4, −6)

       780: (1, 6) and (−4, 2)

21 Ali walked from the library at point (88, 80) to the shop and then onto the pier at point (20, 26). What distance did Adam walk? (3)

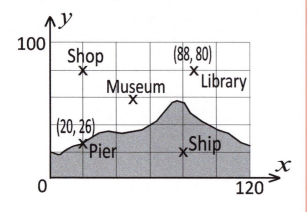

Down:

15 The three points (4, 5), (12, 5) and (4, 21) are the three corners of a right-angled triangle. What is the area of the triangle? (2)

18 The x-coordinate of point P shown below. (2)

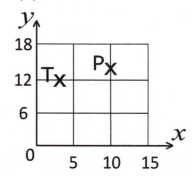

19 The y-coordinate of point T in the diagram shown in 18 down. (2)

Working out:

Working out:

Crossword 26: Transformations

Across:

1 The rectangle on the right is rotated 90° clockwise about (30, 30). What is the new y-coordinate of point Q? (2)

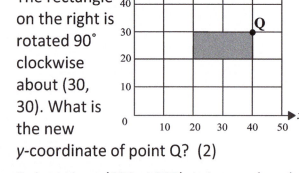

2 Point V is at (900, 1000). It is translated 972 units right and 835 units up. What is its new x-coordinate? (4)

6 Point Q is reflected in the y-axis. A triangle is then formed between points P, the reflected Q and R. What is the area of the triangle? (3)

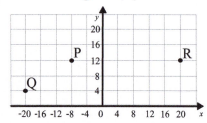

7 Point F is at (−173, 378). It is reflected in the x-axis and then reflected in the y-axis. What is its new x-coordinate? (3)

Down:

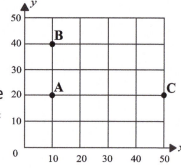

1 Point C on the grid shown is reflected in the vertical line x = 40. Point B is translated 10 units right. A triangle is then formed between points A, B and C. Which randomly numbered answer below describes the triangle? (2)

    21: Obtuse-angled triangle
    25: Right-angled triangle
    29: Acute-angled triangle

3 Point D is at (0, 94). It is translated 11 units down and then rotated 270° anticlockwise about (0, 0). What is its new x-coordinate? (2)

4 The trapezium below is rotated 720° clockwise about its centre. Which of the five randomly numbered trapeziums below show its new position? (3)

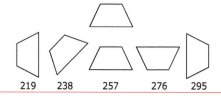

Across:

9 Point P below is reflected in the line L1. It is then reflected in the line L5. Lastly, it is reflected in the line L2. What is the new *x*-coordinate of point P? (2)

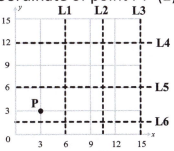

10 This circle is translated 40 units right. What is the *x*-coordinate at its new centre? (2)

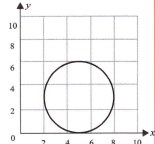

11 Point B at (−517, −577) is reflected in the *x*-axis. What is its new *y*-coordinate? (3)

13 Point C at (0, 15) is rotated 180° anticlockwise about point (10, 15). What is its new *x*-coordinate? (2)

14 Point E on the grid shown is translated 3 units left and 2 units up. What is the area of the new quadrilateral EFGH? (2)

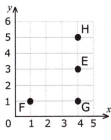

15 The kite below is rotated half a right-angle clockwise about its centre. Which of the five randomly numbered kites below show its new position? (4)

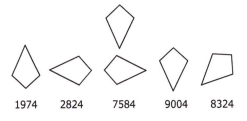

1974   2824   7584   9004   8324

16 Point D at (−3, −19) is translated up 54 units. What is its new *y*-coordinate? (2)

Down:

5 Triangle T below is translated 3 units right. It is then reflected in line M. What is the new *x*-coordinate of point C? (2)

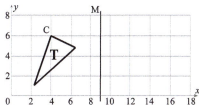

6 Point U at coordinates (0, 50) is translated up 75 units. What is the new *y*-coordinate of point U? (3)

7 A grid is shown below with its axes values in Roman numerals. The line is translated right X Roman numeral units. What is the new numerical *x*-coordinate at the midpoint of the line? (2)

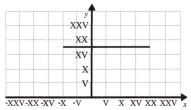

8 Point W on the grid below is rotated 180° clockwise about point (6, 8). It is then moved down 6 units. It is then reflected in the vertical line at *x* = −4 . What is the value (in pence) that point W finishes on? (3)

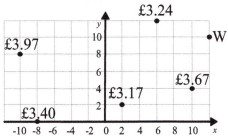

12 Using the grid in clue 8 down, the amount at point (2, 2) is moved 6 units up and 12 units left. It is added to the amount at the coordinates where it finishes. What is the total, in pence? (3)

13 Point C at coordinates (6, 6) is rotated clockwise through a reflex angle about (0, 0) to finish at (−6, 0). What angle is this? (3)

Crossword 27: Symmetry

1			2	3		4	
		5					
6					7		8
				9			
		10	11			12	
	13		14				
15					16		

Across:

1 Part of a regular shape is shown below along with two lines of symmetry. What is the perimeter of the full shape, in cm? (2)

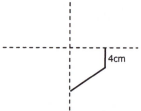

2 What is the result of multiplying the order of rotational symmetry of a regular nonagon by 203? (4)

6 The shapes below are reflected in line M to form a 4 digit number. What is the result of doubling this number? (4)

7 Which randomly numbered answer below represents a correct line of symmetry for the shape? (3)

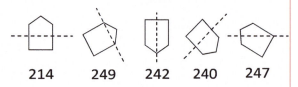

214   249   242   240   247

Down:

1 A shape is shown below along with a line of symmetry. The full shape makes a net of a 3-D shape when folded up. Which of the randomly numbered shapes below is the name of the 3-D shape? (4)

    4,378: Square-based pyramid
    4,219: Triangular prism
    4,062: Tetrahedron
    4,140: Cube

3 What percentage of the letters below have at least one line of symmetry? (2)
    A, H, T, L, I

4 What is the result of multiplying the order of rotational symmetry of a square by 14^2? (3)

5 Part of a shape is shown below along with a line of symmetry. What is the area of the full shape, in mm^2? (4)

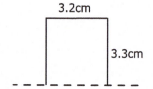

Across:

9 What percentage of the letters below have rotational symmetry of order 2 and line symmetry? (2)

Z, M, K, X, C

10 Some circles are shown below along with a line of symmetry. How many black circles will make up the full diagram? (2)

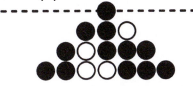

12 How many lines of symmetry are there in total on the shapes below? (2)

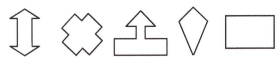

14 Some Roman numerals are shown below. What is the sum of the Roman numerals that have a vertical line of symmetry through their centre? (2)

D, C, V, L, X, X, D

15 What is the result of multiplying the number of lines of symmetry on a regular heptagon by 265? (4)

16 Part of a shape is shown along with a line of symmetry. What is the area of the full shape, in cm^2? (3)

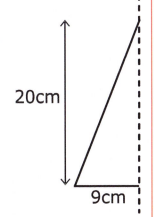

20cm

9cm

Down:

7 What is the sum of the orders of rotational symmetry on the shapes below? (2)

Rhombus
Regular decagon
Equilateral triangle
Regular pentagon

8 The shapes below are reflected in line M to form a Roman numeral. What is its standard number value? (3)

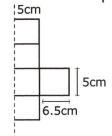

11 A shape is shown below along with a line of symmetry. The full shape makes a net of a 3-D shape when folded up. What is the volume of the shape, in cm^3? (3)

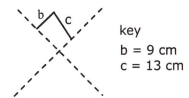

5cm

5cm

6.5cm

12 What is the result of multiplying the number of lines of symmetry on a regular octagon by 16? (3)

13 Part of a shape is shown below along with two lines of symmetry. What is the perimeter of the full shape, in cm? (2)

b c

key
b = 9 cm
c = 13 cm

Crossword 28: Mixed

Across:

1 Two thirds of 381. (3)

3 0.471 tonnes in kilograms. (3)

6 638 rounded to the nearest 10. (3)

7 Range of 81, 57, 209, 57, 108. (3)

8 45% of 160. (2)

10 Solve $2x - 3y$ if $x = 16$ and $y = -13$. (2)

11 Average of 100, 400 and 100. (3)

14 £168 is to be split in the ratio of 5:9 between Liz and Amit. How much in pounds(£) will Liz receive? (2)

15 If 1 gallon ≈ 4 litres, approximately how many gallons are there in 348 litres? (2)

17 Lowest common multiple of 3, 6 and 8. (2)

19 A fair die is thrown 294 times. How many times would you expect the die to land on a 6? (2)

21 What is the volume of a cube in cm^3 that has sides of 4cm? (2)

23 9,696 divided by 12. (3)

Down:

1 How much less is 77 than 18^2? (3)

2 The value of Roman numeral XLVI. (2)

3 4, 40, 400, ? (4)

4 2.75×4 (2)

5 A book costs £26. What is the total cost in pence of two such identical books? (4)

9 How many 10° angles are equivalent to the sum of three right angles? (2)

11 Number of hours in 8.5 days. (3)

12 A square has an area of 4,900mm^2. What is the perimeter of the square, in cm? (2)

13 Combined number of faces on two cubes and five tetrahedrons. (2)

16 Point A at coordinates (25, 83) is translated vertically down 7 units. What is the new y-coordinate of point A? (2)

18 How many days are in 1.2 non-leap years? (3)

Across:

24 A group of people were asked if they had visited the countries in the Venn diagram. How many people had visited more than one of the three countries? (2)

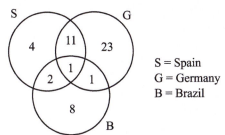

S = Spain
G = Germany
B = Brazil

Down:

20 What is the output of the number machine? (3)

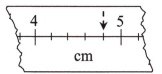

22 What is the reading on the ruler, in mm? (2)

Working out:

Crossword 29: Mixed

Across:

1 The diameter of a circle is 450,000mm. What is its radius, in metres? (3)

3 461.38 + 192.62 (3)

6 What is the input to the number machine below? (3)

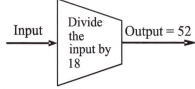

7 What is the numerator of the improper fraction equivalent of the mixed number $126\frac{3}{5}$? (3)

9 1, 3, 6, 10, ? (2)

10 What percentage of these triangles are coloured black? (2)

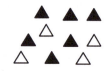

11 The number of lines of symmetry of a regular octagon multiplied by 2. (2)

12 459 divided by 27. (2)

13 The perimeter of a regular nonagon is 234cm. What is the length of one of its sides, in cm? (2)

Down:

2 Point A is at coordinates (−24, 0) and point B is at coordinates (571, 0). What is the number of horizontal units between points A and B? (3)

3 How many seconds are in 111.1 minutes? (4)

4 £92 is to be split in the ratio 3:1 between Kerry and Joe. How many more pounds(£) will Kerry receive than Joe? (2)

5 Sum of 9 squared and the square root of 4. (2)

8 $7^3 - 7^2 + 7$ (3)

9 What is the result of rounding 12.955 to 2 decimal places and then multiplying the answer by 100? (4)

11 If the mean of the following four numbers is 12, what is the value of Y? (2)

    23, −2, 10, Y

13 How many litres in 23,000 millilitres? (2)

Across:

14 45.5 × 8 (3)

17 1418 − 481 (3)

18 What is the probability that $^9/_3 = 3$, expressed as a percentage? (3)

Down:

14 What is the combined score for the five people shown on the chart below? (2)

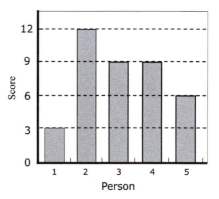

15 Total number of faces on seven pentagonal prisms. (2)

16 The smaller angle(in degrees) between two perpendicular lines? (2)

Working out:

Crossword 30: Mixed

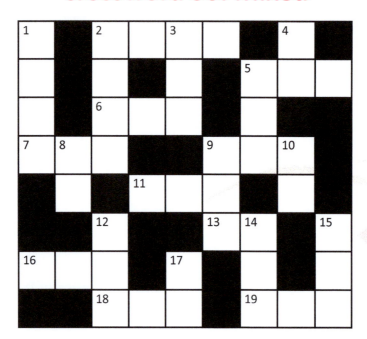

Across:

2   What is the evening time on the clock in 24 hour clock format, written as HHMM? (4)

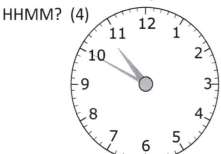

5   What is the size of angle q, in degrees? (3)

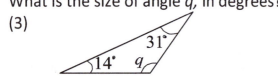

6   1,624 divided by 14. (3)

7   $20^2 + \sqrt{289}$ (3)

9   Median of 135, 130, 7, 131, 135. (3)

11   A cube is 5cm in height. What is its volume, in cm^3? (3)

13   Missing value in the number sequence (2)

     −4500, 900, −180, ? , −7.2

16   An event is 'certain'. What is this expressed as a percentage? (3)

Down:

1   Output of the number machine below. (4)

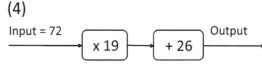

2   What number is equivalent to Roman numerals MMXVII? (4)

3   There are 2780 cards in a shop. There are three different sizes of card (small, medium and large), and the amounts of each are in the ratio 3:5:2. How many large cards are there? (3)

4   If 1 stone ≈ 6kg, approximately how many kilograms are in 10.5 stones? (2)

5   $(198 - 27 + 95) \times 0.5$ (3)

8   A straight line lies between point A at coordinates (−8, 34) and point B at coordinates (−8, −6). What is the y-coordinate at the midpoint of the line? (2)

9   0.85 multiplied by the sum of two right angles, in degrees. (3)

Across:

18 3.2 × 57.5 (3)

19 What is the result of multiplying the number of pairs of parallel sides on a regular octagon by 30? (3)

Down:

10 17.499 rounded to the nearest whole number. (2)

12 8*a* + 362 = 4,370. What is the value of *a*? (3)

14 Increase 376 by 245. (3)

15 Part of a regular shape is shown below along with a line of symmetry. What is the perimeter of the full shape, in mm? (3)

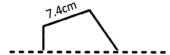
7.4cm

17 Lowest common multiple of 4, 6 and 7. (2)

Working out:

Crossword 31: Mixed

Across:

1 The result of tripling a number is 75. What is the result of multiplying the original number by 7? (3)

3 100.4 multiplied by 2.5. (3)

6 The eighth triangular number multiplied by √144. (3)

7 Millie saw three hundred birds in her garden. The percentages of each bird seen are shown in the pie chart. How many wrens did she see? (2)

Magpies 18%
Robins 13%
Crows 35%
Blackbirds
Wrens

9 What is $^{157}/_{250}$ of 1.5 metres, in mm? (3)

11 How many faces are on 80 octahedrons? (3)

12 Kabir scored the following marks in his spelling tests. What was his average mark? (2)

   14, 18, 3, 16, 9, 6

13 What is the smallest whole number for x that satisfies $x^2 > 95$? (2)

Down:

1 Subtract 87 from 219. (3)

2 Years in half a century. (2)

3 Area of the parallelogram below, in cm^2.(3)

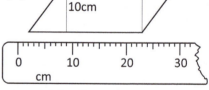

10cm

4 Penny paid for her shopping with a £20 note. She received 600 pence in change. How much did her shopping cost in pounds(£)? (2)

5 If 1 stone = 14 pounds, how many pounds are in 160 stones? (4)

8 A cuboid has length 22cm, height 20cm and breadth 18cm. What is its volume, in cm^3? (4)

10 How many minutes are between quarter past three in the afternoon and 19:10 the same day? (3)

11 77% of £800 in pounds(£). (3)

15 937.5 rounded to the nearest 10. (3)

Across:

14 Point *R* at (84, 85) is translated left 25 units. What is its new *x*-coordinate? (2)

16 1,902 stickers were split between Ruth and Simon in the ratio 2:1. How many more stickers did Ruth get compared to Simon? (3)

19 800, 1000, 1,200, ? (4)

20 Sum of all the factors of 28. (2)

Down:

17 Tom has seven 10p coins, nine 5p coins, thirteen 20p coins and a 1p coin. How much does he have in total, in pence? (3)

18 Size of angle *X* on the kite. (2)

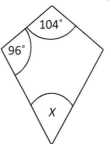

Working out:

Crossword 32: Mixed

1			2		3		
		4				5		6
7	8						
	9		10			11		
					12		
13			14	15		16	17	
		18		19			
	20					21	

Across:

1   What is 28 out of 80 as a percentage? (2)

2   How many more grams need to be added to the scales below to equal 1.681kg? (3)

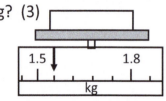

4   Perimeter, in cm, of an equilateral triangle with a side length of $259 \frac{1}{3}$cm. (3)

5   A number machine doubles its input and subtracts 79 from the result. Its input is 507.5, what is its output? (3)

7   Second cube number plus second triangular number. (2)

9   Standard number value of Roman numerals MCCXL. (4)

11   Order of rotational symmetry of a regular hexagon multiplied by 17. (3)

12   132/12 (2)

13   Acute angle between west and northwest. (2)

Down:

1   Sum of 163, 29 and 179. (3)

2   Next value in the sequence below: (4)
0, –100, 450, –200, 900, –300, 1350, –400, ?

3   Point B on the grid below is reflected in the vertical line $x = 20$. It is then translated 50 units down and 20 units right. Which of the randomly numbered answers below describes the direction of point D from the new position of point B? (2)

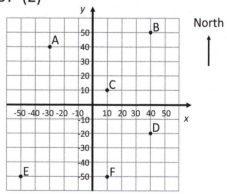

     18: Northwest
     19: Southeast
     21: Southwest
     25: Northeast

6   31 × 22 (3)

Across:

14 $376 + 2x = 562$. Find the value of x (2)

16 A cuboid has a volume of $51,200\text{cm}^3$. Its length is 80cm and its height is 10cm. What is its breadth, in mm? (3)

19 A cube has volume 27cm^3. What is the length of one of its edges, in mm? (2)

20 A fifth of eight thousand one hundred and ten. (4)

21 A pen usually costs £1.20. It is reduced by 25%. How much, in pence, does is it cost now? (2)

Down:

8 Median of 900, 575, 1,800 and 1,450. (4)

10 4.99 metres in centimetres. (3)

11 Number of hours in $4\,^5/_6$ days. (3)

15 332.45 correct to the nearest integer. (3)

17 $(\sqrt{81} + 6^3) \div 0.5$ (3)

18 Total number of vertices on five cubes and six triangular prisms. (2)

Working out:

Crossword 33: Mixed

Across:

1. Next value in the sequence below: (2)
   $47\,^1/_2$, $58\,^5/_8$, $69\,^3/_4$, $80\,^7/_8$, ?

3. Both inputs to the number machine below are > 0. What is the value of input 1? (3)

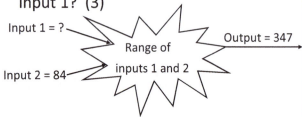

5. Convert $49\,^1/_6$ into an improper fraction and give the numerator of the result. (3)

6. Some squares are shown below along with a dashed line of symmetry. How many shaded squares will make up the full image? (2)

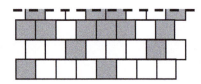

8. Number of minutes between 23:41 on Monday and 01:35 the next day. (3)

Down:

2. If 1 gallon = 8 pints and 1 pint ≈ ½ litre, approximately how many gallons is 896,000 millilitres? (3)

3. Nine thousand, six hundred and sixty-seven minus five thousand and eighty-nine. (4)

4. What is the reading on the scale, in cm? (2)

7. The perimeter of a regular heptagon is 290.64m. What is the length of one of its sides in cm? (4)

9. Convert the Roman numerals MDCCCL to standard number format and round the answer to the nearest 100. (4)

11. Two corner coordinates of a square are (10, 5) and (10, 65). Given that all coordinates at corner points are positive, what is the x-coordinate of the corner point diagonally opposite (10, 5)? (2)

Across:

10 Number of edges on three octagonal prisms. (2)

11 Three interior angles in an irregular quadrilateral are 156°, 74° and 52°. What is the size of the other interior angle? (2)

12 80.5 represents 25% of what value? (3)

14 $189 - 2y = 11y - 3724$. What is the value of y? (3)

17 $1296 \div 2.7$ (3)

Down:

13 Alan bought six plastic containers each holding three tennis balls at a price of £8 per container. He also bought three plastic containers, each holding four tennis balls at a price of £10 per container. How much did he spend on average per tennis ball, in pence? (3)

15 Highest common factor of 42 and 98 (2)

16 Dajana has four £2 coins, five £1 coins, ten 50p coins, six 20p coins, one 10p coin and twelve 5p coins in her purse. She selects a coin at random, what is the probability, as a percentage, that it is worth at least 50p? (2)

Working out:

Crossword 34: Mixed

Across:

1   Output of the number machine below if the input is 6. (3)

Input → $\div 2$ → $+ 5^2$ → $\times 19$ → Output

3   What is the difference between 7620 and 8309? (3)

5   Marilyn has five 885ml bottles full of water and eight 1.5 litre bottles full of water. How many millilitres short of 17 litres of water is she? (3)

7   Next value in the sequence below: (2)
    12.25, 12.6, 12.95, 13.3, 13.65, ?

8   Julian had 20 hats. He increased his hat collection by 30%. How many hats does he now have? (2)

9   What is the sum of the median and mode values of the numbers below? (2)
        53, –4, 5, 90, 57, –4, 0, 68, 49

10 £162 was split in the ratio of 4:5 between Soulla and Raul. How many pounds short of £114 was Raul after he received his share? (2)

Down:

1   A circle has a diameter of 10.86 metres. What is its radius in centimetres? (3)

2   A letter is chosen at random from the word PROPORTIONAL. What is the probability, as a percentage, the letter is an O? (2)

3   A right-angled triangle has an area of 4,225mm^2. Its base is half of its height. What is its base, in mm? (2)

4   47.2 × 20   (3)

6   65 rounded to the nearest 10. (2)

7   Josephine went on holiday on Friday 27th May for 30 days, excluding the day she left. Which randomly numbered answer below is the day of the week she returned? (2)
        13 Friday
        18 Wednesday
        16 Saturday
        15 Sunday
        11 Monday

Across:

12 What is the product of the first square number, the second cube number, the third prime number and the fourth triangular number? (3)

13 The four shapes below have random numbers underneath them. Which random number is associated with the square-based pyramid? (3)

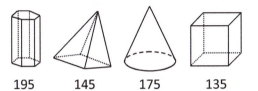

195   145   175   135

Down:

8   Three sevenths of 490. (3)

9   The perimeter of a square is 84cm. What is its area, in cm^2? (3)

11 What is the value of k below, in degrees? (2)

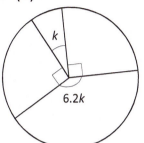

Working out:

Crossword 35: Worded

Fill in the crossword and the grey squares will spell out the name of a common 2D shape.

Across:

1 Imperial unit of weight equivalent to 2,240 pounds. (3)

3 US currency equal to 100 cents. (6)

7 Examples of these include 1:3 and 5:2:1 and they define the relationship between the sizes of two or more values. (6)

8 Curved shape resembling an ellipse. (4)

10 Common 3D shape with four or five vertices depending on type. (7)

12 Term describing a collection of data with two modes. (7)

16 ____ chance, equal probability of occurring. (4)

17 Basic unit of an angle. (6)

18 Units of capacity. (6)

19 To sum. (3)

Down:

1 A triangular number. (5)

2 Flat figures that can be folded up to form 3D shapes. (4)

4 The number 68 in Roman numerals. (6)

5 An instruction followed to help solve maths problems. (4)

6 A 2D shape with three or more straight sides. (7)

9 A collection of numbers or information. (7)

11 To cut or divide into two equal parts. (6)

13 Measured as distance travelled per unit of time. (5)

14 A single boxed area in a row or column of a table. (4)

15 Amount of 2D space taken up by an object. (4)

FIRST PAST THE POST®

Answers

75

Crossword 1: Addition and Subtraction

1 **1**	■	2 **2**	■	3 **1**	**4**	4 **7**	■	5 **6**
1	■	6 **8**	**7**	**2**	■	7 **7**	**1**	**0**
8 **1**	9 **9**	■	■	**0**	■	12 **2**	■	**8**
■	10 **6**	**2**	11 **6**	■	■	12 **2**	**6**	**5**
■	■	■	**0**	■	13 **5**	**0**	■	■
14 **5**	15 **1**	■	16 **4**	17 **7**	■	18 **4**	19 **9**	■
■	20 **1**	21 **7**	■	**1**	■	■	**4**	■
■	22 **2**	**0**	**4**	■	23 **2**	**9**	**3**	■

Crossword 2: Multiplication and Division

1 **2**	**4**	2 **2**	■	3 **4**	**0**	4 **2**	■	5 **3**
8	■	**3**	■	**2**	■	6 **8**	**5**	**0**
■	7 **4**	■	8 **3**	■	■	■	■	**0**
■	9 **9**	**5**	**4**	**1**	■	10 **8**	**8**	**0**
■	**7**	■	**5**	■	11 **8**	**4**	■	■
12 **1**	**6**	■	13 **6**	14 **9**	■	15 **8**	16 **7**	■
■	■	17 **5**	■	**1**	■	■	18 **2**	**8**
■	19 **1**	**0**	**1**	**5**	■	20 **9**	**9**	■

Crossword 3: Mixed Operations

Crossword 4: Number Value

Crossword 5: Factors and Multiples

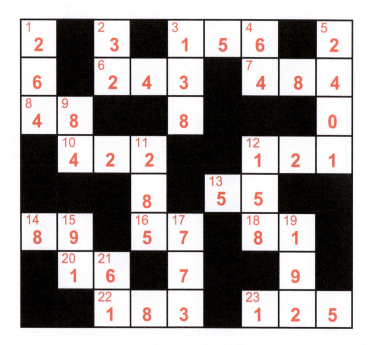

Crossword 6: Number Sequences

Crossword 7: Decimal Numbers

Crossword 8: Special Numbers

Crossword 9: Number Machines

Crossword 10: Algebra

Crossword 11: Fractions and Mixed Numbers

1		2		3		4		5
1		1		1	6	5		3
3		6 5	1	9		7 2	7	3
8 5	9 4			0				0
	10 2	5	11 2			12 4	4	0
			2		13 3	2		
14 4	15 6		16 4	17 9		18 1	19 3	
	20 5	21 8		8			9	
		22 1	4	8		23 5	0	0

Crossword 12: Percentages

Crossword 13: Ratio

Crossword 14: Representing Data

Crossword 15: Mean, Median, Mode and Range

Crossword 16: Probability

Crossword 17: Reading Scales

¹2	6	■	²2	³6	1	⁴2	■
4	■	⁵3	■	6	■	4	■
■	⁶1	9	2	■	⁷2	0	⁸5
⁹3	4	■	■	¹⁰3	0	■	6
■	0	■	¹¹4	0	■	■	0
¹²3	0	¹³8	■	0	■	¹⁴7	0
■	■	4	■	0	■	1	■

Crossword 18: Length, Weight and Capacity

¹1	0	²2	■	³7	6	⁴1	■	⁵4
1	■	8	■	0	■	⁶7	9	4
■	⁷3	■	⁸5	■	■	■	■	0
■	⁹1	2	3	2	■	¹⁰5	4	0
■	2	■	0	■	¹¹1	2	■	■
¹²2	4	■	¹³1	¹⁴9	■	¹⁵6	¹⁶8	■
■	¹⁷4	■	■	4	■	■	¹⁸7	3
■	¹⁹1	2	7	0	■	²⁰1	5	■

Crossword 19: Dates, Time and Timetables

1 1	■	2 2	2	3 1	8	■	4 3	■
9	■	0	■	2	■	5 3	4	5
1	■	6 4	9	2	■	7	■	■
7 8	8 2	5	■	■	9 1	8	10 1	■
■	9	■	11 2	0	0	■	12 2	13 4
■	14 1	■	■	■	15 7	16 9	■	3
17 1	0	2	■	18 6	■	4	■	2
■	19 6	0	0	0	9	■	■	0

Crossword 20: Lines, Angles and Bearings

Crossword 21: 2-D Shapes

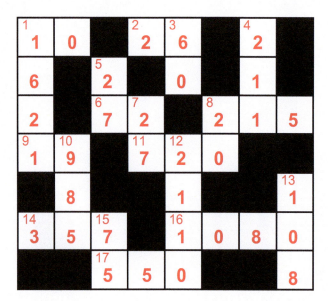

Crossword 22: Perimeter and Area

Crossword 23: 3-D Shapes

Crossword 24: Volume

Crossword 25: Co-ordinates

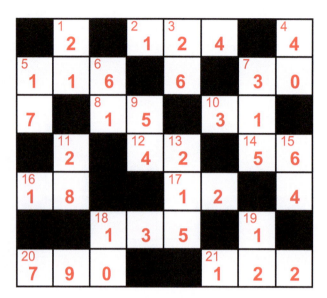

Crossword 26: Transformations

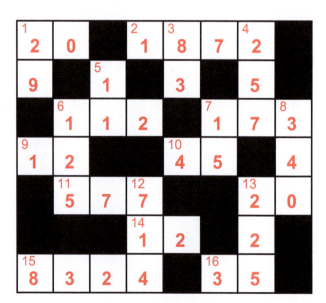

Crossword 27: Symmetry

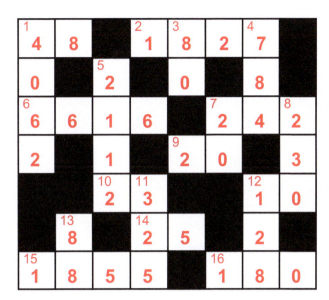

Crossword 28: Mixed

Crossword 29: Mixed

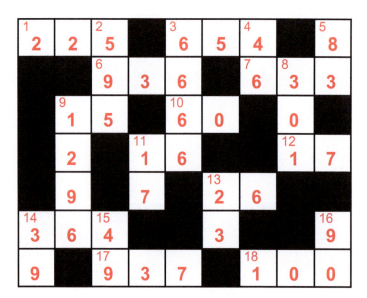

Crossword 30: Mixed

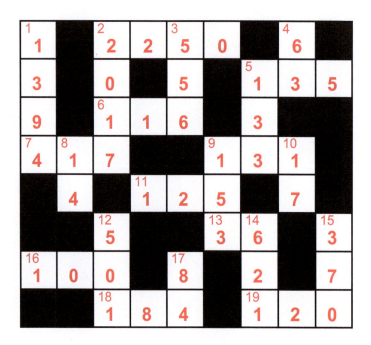

Crossword 31: Mixed

1:1	7	2:5	■	3:2	5	4:1	■	5:2
3	■	0		1	■	6:4	3	2
7:2	8:7	■		0	■			4
■	9:9	4	10:2	■		11:6	4	0
	2	■	3		12:1	1	■	
13:1	0	■	14:5	15:9	■	16:6	17:3	4
■	18:6	■	4		■		7	■
19:1	4	0	0	■		20:5	6	■

Crossword 32: Mixed

1:3	5	■		2:1	2	3:1	■
7	■	4:7	7	8	■	5:9	3	6:6
7:1	8:1	■		0	■			8
■	9:1	2	10:4	0	■	11:1	0	2
	7	■	9	■	12:1	1	■	
13:4	5	■	14:9	15:3	■	16:6	17:4	0
■	18:7	■	19:3	0	■		5	■
20:1	6	2	2	■	21:9	0	

Crossword 33: Mixed

Crossword 34: Mixed

Crossword 35: Worded

Mystery Shape: TRIANGLE

Working out: